PICNIC

A PICNIC COOKBOOK WITH DELICIOUS PICNIC IDEAS

By
BookSumo Press
Copyright © by Saxonberg Associates
All rights reserved

Published by
BookSumo Press, a DBA of Saxonberg Associates
http://www.booksumo.com/

About the Author.

BookSumo Press is a publisher of unique, easy, and healthy cookbooks.

Our cookbooks span all topics and all subjects. If you want a deep dive into the possibilities of cooking with any type of ingredient. Then BookSumo Press is your go to place for robust yet simple and delicious cookbooks and recipes. Whether you are looking for great tasting pressure cooker recipes or authentic ethic and cultural food. BookSumo Press has a delicious and easy cookbook for you.

With simple ingredients, and even simpler step-by-step instructions BookSumo cookbooks get everyone in the kitchen chefing delicious meals.

BookSumo is an independent publisher of books operating in the beautiful Garden State (NJ) and our team of chefs and kitchen experts are here to teach, eat, and be merry!

INTRODUCTION

Welcome to *The Effortless Chef Series*! Thank you for taking the time to purchase this cookbook.

Come take a journey into the delights of easy cooking. The point of this cookbook and all BookSumo Press cookbooks is to exemplify the effortless nature of cooking simply.

In this book we focus on Picnic. You will find that even though the recipes are simple, the taste of the dishes are quite amazing.

So will you take an adventure in simple cooking? If the answer is yes please consult the table of contents to find the dishes you are most interested in.

Once you are ready, jump right in and start cooking.

— BookSumo Press

TABLE OF CONTENTS

About the Author 2

Introduction 3

Table of Contents 4

Any Issues? Contact Us 9

Legal Notes 10

Common Abbreviations 11

Chapter 1: Muffins & Breads 12

    Autumn Picnic Apple Muffins 12

    Honey Graham Muffins 14

    Grape Muffins for a Sweet Day 16

    Cranberry Muffins 18

    Blueberry Muffins 20

    Honey Spelt Bread 22

    Picnic Pumpernickel Bread 24

    Rich Cinnamon Bread 26

    Homemade White Bread 28

    Picnic Parsley Garlic Bread 30

Chapter 2: Sandwiches 32

    Easy Rustic Apple Sandwich 32

    Peanut and Olive Sandwich 34

    Pepper Beef Sandwich 36

Beef Broiled Sandwich 38

Tandoori Apple Asiago Sandwich 40

Crab Salad Sandwich 42

Tuna Sandwiches 44

Hawaiian Tuna Sandwiches 46

Easy Slow Cooker Pulled Pork Sandwiches 48

The Tropical Sandwich 50

Parmigiano-Reggiano Sandwich 52

Chapter 3: Hot Dogs 54

Windy City Chicago Hot Dogs 54

American Picnic Hot Dogs 56

The Simplest Hot Dogs 58

Austrian Style Hot Dogs 60

Manhattan Island Hot Dog Topping 62

Minnesota Style Hot Dogs 64

How to Make An American Hot Dog 66

Summer Backyard Hot Dogs 68

Brooklyn Style Hot Dogs 70

Gourmet Hot Dogs 72

Chapter 4: French Fries 74

Georgia Backroad Fries 74

New Jersey Diner Style Fries 76

French Fry Dinner Bake 78

Simple Portuguese Inspired Fries 80

Elegant Truffle Oil and Parsley Fries 82

    Seasoned Crinkle Cuts 84

    How to Bake French Fries 86

    Louisiana Creole Fries 88

    Easy Aztec Style Fries 90

    Indian Style Curry Cumin Fries 92

Chapter 5: Coleslaw 94

    6 Ingredient Coleslaw 94

    Dijon Raisin Coleslaw 96

    Mexican Style Coleslaw 98

    Coleslaw Crossroads 100

    San Antonio Coleslaw 102

    Buttermilk Coleslaw 104

    Autumn Picnic Coleslaw 106

    Hawaiian Coleslaw 108

    Apple Cider Grapeseed Coleslaw 110

    Garden Fresh Coleslaw 112

Chapter 6: Fried Chicken 114

    Crispy Garlicky Fried Chicken 114

    Cheesy Parsley Parmesan Oven Fried Chicken 116

    Buttermilk Paprika Fried Chicken 118

    6-Ingredient Fried Chicken 120

    Indian Style Fried Chicken 122

    Crispy Fried Chicken Croquettes 124

    Oriental Fried Chicken Thighs 127

    Kanas Style Fried Chicken Cutlets 129

Fried Chicken In A Japanese Style ... 131
Fried Chicken with Honey Nut Sauce ... 133

Chapter 7: Salads ... 135

American Potato Salad ... 135

Egg Salad ... 137

Chicken Salad ... 139

Corn Salad ... 141

Ensalada de Papas Colombiana (10-Ingredient Potato Salad) ... 143

Tuna Salad ... 145

Macaroni Salad ... 147

Mesa Macaroni Salad ... 149

Maque Choux (Native American Style Corn Salad) ... 151

Ceviche Guatemala Style ... 153

Chapter 8: Burgers and Veggie Burgers ... 155

White Steak Burgers ... 155

Grilled Mozzarella Burger ... 157

Chili Romano Burgers ... 159

Grilled Cottage Sandwich ... 161

Braggs' Oat Burgers ... 163

Dreamy Cheesy Burger ... 165

Peanut Butter Burgers ... 167

Barbecue Oat Burgers ... 169

Hot Chili Braggs Burgers ... 171

Yoshida Burgers ... 173

Latin Salsa Burgers ... 175

Worcestershire Pastrami Burger	177
Quaker Corn Burgers	179
Classical London Sirloin Burger	181
Appendix I: Spice Mixes	183
Mango & Raisin Chutney	183
Cajun Spice Mix	185
THANKS FOR READING! JOIN THE CLUB AND KEEP ON COOKING WITH 6 MORE COOKBOOKS....	187
Come On...	189
Let's Be Friends :)	189

Any Issues? Contact Us

If you find that something important to you is missing from this book please contact us at info@booksumo.com.

We will take your concerns into consideration when the 2nd edition of this book is published. And we will keep you updated!

— BookSumo Press

LEGAL NOTES

ALL RIGHTS RESERVED. NO PART OF THIS BOOK MAY BE REPRODUCED OR TRANSMITTED IN ANY FORM OR BY ANY MEANS. PHOTOCOPYING, POSTING ONLINE, AND / OR DIGITAL COPYING IS STRICTLY PROHIBITED UNLESS WRITTEN PERMISSION IS GRANTED BY THE BOOK'S PUBLISHING COMPANY. LIMITED USE OF THE BOOK'S TEXT IS PERMITTED FOR USE IN REVIEWS WRITTEN FOR THE PUBLIC.

Common Abbreviations

cup(s)	C.
tablespoon	tbsp
teaspoon	tsp
ounce	oz.
pound	lb

*All units used are standard American measurements

Chapter 1: Muffins & Breads

Autumn Picnic Apple Muffins

Ingredients

- 2 1/2 C. all-purpose flour
- 2 C. white sugar
- 1 tbsp pumpkin pie spice
- 1 tsp baking soda
- 1/2 tsp salt
- 2 eggs, lightly beaten
- 1 C. canned pumpkin puree
- 1/2 C. vegetable oil
- 2 C. peeled, cored and chopped apple
- 2 tbsp all-purpose flour
- 1/4 C. white sugar
- 1/2 tsp ground cinnamon
- 4 tsp butter

Directions

- Set your oven to 350 degrees F before doing anything else and lightly, grease 18 cups of muffin trays. In a large bowl, sift together 2 1/2 C. of the flour, baking soda, 2 C. of the sugar, pumpkin pie spice and salt. In another bowl, add the eggs, oil and pumpkin and beat till well combined. Add the egg mixture into the flour mixture and mix till well combined. Fold in the apples and transfer the mixture onto the prepared muffin cups evenly.
- In another bowl, mix together the remaining flour, sugar and cinnamon. With a pastry cutter, cut the butter and mix till a coarse crumb forms. Place the mixture over each muffin evenly and cook everything in the oven for about 35-40 minutes or till a toothpick inserted in the center comes out clean.

Amount per serving (18 total)

Timing Information:

Preparation	15 m
Cooking	45 m
Total Time	1 h

Nutritional Information:

Calories	249 kcal
Fat	8 g
Carbohydrates	42.6g
Protein	2.8 g
Cholesterol	23 mg
Sodium	182 mg

* Percent Daily Values are based on a 2,000 calorie diet.

Honey Graham Muffins

Ingredients

- 2 1/2 C. graham cracker crumbs
- 1/4 C. white sugar
- 2 tsp baking powder
- 1 C. whole milk
- 1 egg, slightly beaten
- 2 tbsp honey

Directions

- Set your oven to 400 degrees F before doing anything else and grease 10 C. of a muffin tin.
- In a bowl, mix together the cracker crumbs, sugar and baking powder.
- Add the egg, milk and honey and mix till well combined.
- Place the mixture into the prepared muffin tin.
- Cook everything in the oven for about 15-18 minutes or till a toothpick inserted in the center comes out clean.
- Remove everything from the oven and keep aside to cool completely.

Amount per serving (10 total)

Timing Information:

Preparation	10 m
Cooking	18 m
Total Time	30 m

Nutritional Information:

Calories	143 kcal
Fat	3.4 g
Carbohydrates	25.9g
Protein	2.9 g
Cholesterol	21 mg
Sodium	216 mg

* Percent Daily Values are based on a 2,000 calorie diet.

Grape Muffins for a Sweet Day

Ingredients

- 2 1/2 C. flour
- 1 C. sugar
- 2 1/2 tsp baking powder
- 1 C. milk
- 1 tsp vanilla
- 2 eggs, well beaten
- 1/2 C. butter, melted
- 1 1/2 C. red seedless grapes, cut into pieces

Directions

- Set your oven to 375 degrees F before doing anything else and line 12 cups of a muffin tin with paper liners.
- In a large bowl, mix together the flour, baking powder and sugar.
- Make a well in the center of the flour mixture and add the eggs, milk, butter and vanilla and mix till well combined.
- Fold in the grapes and transfer the mixture into prepared muffin cups.
- Cook everything in the oven for about 25 minutes.

Amount per serving: 12

Timing Information:

Preparation	15 mins
Total Time	40 mins

Nutritional Information:

Calories	266.5
Fat	9.4g
Cholesterol	54.1mg
Sodium	166.0mg
Carbohydrates	41.2g
Protein	4.6g

* Percent Daily Values are based on a 2,000 calorie diet.

Cranberry Muffins

Ingredients

- 1 1/2 C. all-purpose flour
- 3 tsps baking powder
- Salt, to taste
- 1/4 C. vegetable oil
- 1/4 C. white sugar
- 1 egg
- 1 C. fresh orange juice
- 1 1/2 C. cranberries, chopped
- 1 tbsp fresh orange zest, grated finely

Directions:

- Set your oven to 400 degrees before doing anything else.
- Grease and flour a 12 C. muffin tin.
- In a large bowl, mix together the flour, baking powder and salt.
- In another bowl, add the oil and sugar and beat till light.
- Add the egg and orange juice and beat till well combined.
- Add the egg mixture into the flour mixture and mix till well combined also.
- Fold in the cranberries and orange zest.
- Place the mixture into the prepared muffin C. about 2/3 of full.
- Bake everything for about 20-25 minutes or till a toothpick inserted in the center comes out clean.

Amount per serving (12 total)

Timing Information:

Preparation	10 m
Cooking	30 m
Total Time	40 m

Nutritional Information:

Calories	136 kcal
Fat	5.2 g
Carbohydrates	20.4g
Protein	2.3 g
Cholesterol	16 mg
Sodium	177 mg

* Percent Daily Values are based on a 2,000 calorie diet.

Blueberry Muffins

Ingredients

- 2 C. all-purpose flour
- 2 tsps baking powder
- Salt, to taste
- 1 1/2 C. white sugar, divided
- 1/2 C. butter, softened
- 2 eggs
- 1/4 C. milk
- 1/2 C. fresh blueberries, mashed
- 2 C. fresh blueberries

Directions:

- Set your oven to 375 degrees before doing anything else.
- Grease and flour an 18 C. muffin tin.
- In a large bowl, mix together the flour, baking powder and salt.
- In another bowl, add 1 1/4 C. of sugar and butter and beat till light.
- Add the eggs, one at a time and beat till well combined.
- Add the egg mixture into the flour mixture and mix till well combined.
- Add the milk and mix well.
- Add the mashed blueberries and mix well.
- Fold in the fresh blueberries.
- Place the mixture into prepared muffin C. so that about 2/3 of each section is full.
- Dust with the remaining sugar.
- Bake everything for about 30 minutes or till a toothpick inserted in the center comes out clean.

Amount per serving (18 total)

Timing Information:

Preparation	10 m
Cooking	40 m
Total Time	50 m

Nutritional Information:

Calories	182 kcal
Fat	5.9 g
Carbohydrates	30.5g
Protein	2.4 g
Cholesterol	34 mg
Sodium	165 mg

* Percent Daily Values are based on a 2,000 calorie diet.

Honey Spelt Bread

Ingredients

- 1 C. water
- 1 1/2 tsp vegetable oil
- 1 1/2 tsp honey
- 1/2 tsp lecithin
- 3 C. white spelt flour
- 3 tbsp dry milk powder
- 1 1/2 tsp salt
- 2 tsp active dry yeast

Directions

- In the bread machine pan, place all the ingredients in the order recommended by the manufacturer.
- Set the Normal or Basic cycle and press Start.

Amount per serving (12 total)

Timing Information:

Preparation	10 m
Cooking	1 h
Total Time	1 h 30 m

Nutritional Information:

Calories	118 kcal
Fat	1.3 g
Carbohydrates	23g
Protein	4.9 g
Cholesterol	1 mg
Sodium	302 mg

* Percent Daily Values are based on a 2,000 calorie diet.

Picnic Pumpernickel Bread

Ingredients

- 1 1/8 C. warm water
- 1 1/2 tbsp vegetable oil
- 1/3 C. molasses
- 3 tbsp cocoa
- 1 tbsp caraway seed (optional)
- 1 1/2 tsp salt
- 1 1/2 C. bread flour
- 1 C. rye flour
- 1 C. whole wheat flour
- 1 1/2 tbsp vital wheat gluten (optional)
- 2 1/2 tsp bread machine yeast

Directions

- In the bread machine pan, place all the ingredients in the order recommended by the manufacturer.
- Set the Basic cycle and press Start.

Amount per serving (12 total)

Timing Information:

Preparation	10 m
Cooking	3 h 45 m
Total Time	3 h 55 m

Nutritional Information:

Calories	181 kcal
Fat	2.6 g
Carbohydrates	34.8g
Protein	5.5 g
Cholesterol	0 mg
Sodium	296 mg

* Percent Daily Values are based on a 2,000 calorie diet.

Rich Cinnamon Bread

Ingredients

- 7 fluid oz. warm water (110 degrees F/45 degrees C)
- 2 tbsp lard
- 1 (.25 oz.) package active dry yeast
- 2 3/4 C. bread flour
- 1 tsp salt
- 1 tsp ground cinnamon (optional)

Directions

- In the bread machine pan, place the warm water and lard.
- Sprinkle with the yeast.
- Place the flour, salt and toss in the cinnamon.
- Select the cycle and press Start.

Amount per serving (10 total)

Timing Information:

Preparation	5 m
Cooking	2 h 55 m
Total Time	3 h

Nutritional Information:

Calories	162 kcal
Fat	3.2 g
Carbohydrates	27.8g
Protein	4.8 g
Cholesterol	2 mg
Sodium	234 mg

* Percent Daily Values are based on a 2,000 calorie diet.

Homemade White Bread

Ingredients

- 1 C. warm water (110 degrees F/45 degrees C)
- 3 tbsp white sugar
- 1 1/2 tsp salt
- 3 tbsp vegetable oil
- 3 C. bread flour
- 2 1/4 tsp active dry yeast

Directions

- In the bread machine pan, place all the ingredients in the order recommended by the manufacturer.
- Select the White Bread setting.
- Cool on wire racks before slicing.

Amount per serving (12 total)

Timing Information:

Preparation	5 m
Cooking	3 h
Total Time	3 h 5 m

Nutritional Information:

Calories	168 kcal
Fat	4 g
Carbohydrates	28.3g
Protein	4.4 g
Cholesterol	0 mg
Sodium	292 mg

* Percent Daily Values are based on a 2,000 calorie diet.

Picnic Parsley Garlic Bread

Ingredients

- 1 C. warm water (110 degrees F)
- 1 tbsp butter
- 1 tbsp dry milk powder
- 1 tbsp white sugar
- 1 1/2 tsp salt
- 1 1/2 tbsp dried parsley
- 2 tsp garlic powder
- 3 C. bread flour
- 2 tsp active dry yeast

Directions

- In the bread machine pan, place all the ingredients in the order recommended by the manufacturer.
- Select the Basic Bread cycle and press Start.

Amount per serving (12 total)

Timing Information:

Preparation	10 m
Cooking	30 m
Total Time	3 h 10 m

Nutritional Information:

Calories	142 kcal
Fat	1.6 g
Carbohydrates	26.9g
Protein	4.7 g
Cholesterol	3 mg
Sodium	303 mg

* Percent Daily Values are based on a 2,000 calorie diet.

Chapter 2: Sandwiches

Easy Rustic Apple Sandwich

Ingredients

- 1 tbsp butter
- 2 slices bread
- 3 tbsps applesauce

Directions

- Coat 1 side of the bread with butter then place the buttered portion of the bread facing downwards in a hot frying pan.
- Coat the top of the bread with your applesauce evenly and cook the bread for 6 mins after forming a sandwich between the two pieces.
- Enjoy.

Amount per serving (1 total)

Timing Information:

Preparation	Cooking	Total Time
5 m	5 m	10 m

Nutritional Information:

Calories	254 kcal
Fat	13.2 g
Carbohydrates	30.5g
Protein	4 g
Cholesterol	31 mg
Sodium	423 mg

* Percent Daily Values are based on a 2,000 calorie diet.

Peanut and Olive Sandwich

Ingredients

- 2 tbsps peanut butter
- 2 slices bread
- 8 green olives, sliced

Directions

- Coat 1 piece of bread with peanut butter then evenly with your olives.
- Form a sandwich with the other piece of bread.
- Enjoy.

Amount per serving (1 total)

Timing Information:

Preparation	Cooking	Total Time
	10 m	10 m

Nutritional Information:

Calories	360 kcal
Fat	22 g
Carbohydrates	32.1g
Protein	12.4 g
Cholesterol	0 mg
Sodium	1239 mg

* Percent Daily Values are based on a 2,000 calorie diet.

Pepper Beef Sandwich

Ingredients

- 5 lbs chuck roast
- 2 cubes beef bouillon
- 2 tbsps salt
- 2 tsps garlic salt
- 2 bay leaves
- 2 tbsps whole black peppercorns
- 2 tsps dried oregano
- 1 1/2 tsps dried rosemary

Directions

- Submerge your chuck in water.
- Add in the garlic salt, regular salt and bouillon.
- Stir in the spices evenly then add the following to a coffee filter: rosemary, bay leaves, oregano, and peppercorns.
- Seal the spices in the filter with a rubber band and place the bundle into the water with the chuck.
- Get everything boiling, set the heat to low, place a lid on the pot, and let the chuck cook for 7 hrs.
- Throw away the bundle of spices and place the meat to the side to lose some of heat.
- After the chuck has cooled shred it into pieces and serve the meat on toasted rolls.
- When serving your chuck top the meat liberally with the broth.
- Enjoy.

Amount per serving (5 total)

Timing Information:

Preparation	Cooking	Total Time
20 m	7 h	7 h 20 m

Nutritional Information:

Calories	934 kcal
Fat	61.1 g
Carbohydrates	2.5g
Protein	< 87.9 g
Cholesterol	1295 mg
Sodium	4110 mg

* Percent Daily Values are based on a 2,000 calorie diet.

Beef Broiled Sandwich

Ingredients

- 1 C. chopped cooked beef
- 2 stalks celery, chopped
- 1 carrot, diced
- 1/4 C. chopped onion
- 3 tbsps mayonnaise
- 1/4 tsp salt
- 1/8 tsp ground black pepper
- 1/8 tsp garlic powder
- 2 sesame seed buns, toasted until the broiler

Directions

- Get a bowl, combine: garlic powder, beef, black pepper, celery, salt, carrot, mayo, and onion. Stir the mix until it is even.
- Enjoy on toasted sesame seed buns.

Amount per serving (4 total)

Timing Information:

Preparation	Cooking	Total Time
	15 m	15 m

Nutritional Information:

Calories	228 kcal
Fat	17.8 g
Carbohydrates	3.4g
Protein	13.2 g
Cholesterol	46 mg
Sodium	261 mg

* Percent Daily Values are based on a 2,000 calorie diet.

Tandoori Apple Asiago Sandwich

Ingredients

- 1 apple, cored and chopped
- 1/3 bunch kale, chopped
- 1 tbsp tandoori seasoning
- 1 tsp cayenne pepper
- 1/4 C. apple cider
- 1 tbsp olive oil
- 4 slices bacon
- 3 large cracked wheat dinner-style rolls, split
- 3 tbsps grated Asiago cheese

Directions

- Fry your bacon for 11 mins then place the bacon on some paper towel to drain.
- Begin to stir the following in the apple cider, apples, cayenne, kale, and tandoori spice.
- Top the mix with the olive oil as it fries in the bacon fat and let everything cook for 8 mins. Then place the mix to the side.
- Evenly coat the bottom piece of the bread with the tandoori mix then with some bacon and asiago.
- Form sandwiches with the other half of the bread.
- Enjoy.

Amount per serving (3 total)

Timing Information:

Preparation	Cooking	Total Time
15 m	15 m	30 m

Nutritional Information:

Calories	342 kcal
Fat	21.9 g
Carbohydrates	30.5g
Protein	9.5 g
Cholesterol	26 mg
Sodium	492 mg

* Percent Daily Values are based on a 2,000 calorie diet.

Crab Salad Sandwich

Ingredients

- 1 (8 oz.) package imitation crab or lobster meat
- 1/4 C. mayonnaise
- 1 tbsp finely chopped red onion
- 1 tsp lemon juice
- 1/4 tsp seafood Seasoning
- 1 tbsp butter, softened
- 2 hot dog buns

Directions

- Get a bowl, combine: seafood seasoning, crab (flaked), lemon juice, mayo, and onions.
- Place a covering of plastic around the bowl and put everything in the oven for 35 mins.
- Now get your oven's broiler hot before continuing
- Place your buns in a broiler pan after coating them with the butter.
- Broil the bread until it is nicely toasted for a few mins then top each one evenly with the crab salad.
- Enjoy.

Amount per serving (2 total)

Timing Information:

Preparation	Cooking	Total Time
15 m	5 m	50 m

Nutritional Information:

Calories	478 kcal
Fat	30 g
Carbohydrates	39.7g
Protein	13 g
Cholesterol	48 mg
Sodium	1413 mg

* Percent Daily Values are based on a 2,000 calorie diet.

Tuna Sandwiches

Ingredients

- 1 (6 oz.) can tuna, drained
- 1/4 C. mayonnaise
- 1 1/2 tsps cream-style horseradish sauce
- 1 tbsp chopped dill pickles
- 2 leaves lettuce
- 2 slices Swiss cheese
- 4 slices bread
- 2 slices tomato
- 2 thin slices red onion

Directions

- Get a bowl, combine: pickles, tuna, horseradish, and mayo. Stir the mix until it even and smooth.
- Top 2 pieces of bread with 1 piece of Swiss and a piece of lettuce. Evenly divide your tuna mix between the bread slices then layer your onions and tomatoes.
- Place the other piece of bread to make a sandwich.
- Enjoy.

Amount per serving (2 total)

Timing Information:

Preparation	Cooking	Total Time
	15 m	15 m

Nutritional Information:

Calories	553 kcal
Fat	32.9 g
Carbohydrates	30.2g
Protein	33.7 g
Cholesterol	63 mg
Sodium	656 mg

* Percent Daily Values are based on a 2,000 calorie diet.

Hawaiian Tuna Sandwiches

Ingredients

- 4 hamburger buns, split
- 2 tbsps butter
- 1 (6 oz.) can tuna chunks in olive oil
- 1 tbsp lemon juice
- salt and freshly ground black pepper to taste
- 1 dash chili powder
- 1 C. shredded lettuce
- 1 C. shredded mozzarella cheese
- 4 canned pineapple rings

Directions

- Set your oven to 350 degrees before doing anything else.
- Toast the buns under the broiler then coat the insides with some butter.
- Remove 1/2 of the oil from your cans of tuna then place the tuna in a bowl with: chili powder, lemon juice, pepper, and salt.
- Stir the mix to evenly distribute the spices then divide the mix between your toasted buns.
- Now place the following on top: 1 piece of pineapple, some lettuce, and mozzarella.
- Form the sandwiches and place them on a cookie sheet.
- Put the sandwiches in the oven for 11 mins or until you find the cheese has melted.
- Enjoy.

Amount per serving (4 total)

Timing Information:

Preparation	Cooking	Total Time
10 m	15 m	25 m

Nutritional Information:

Calories	369 kcal
Fat	16 g
Carbohydrates	32.5g
Protein	23 g
Cholesterol	41 mg
Sodium	613 mg

* Percent Daily Values are based on a 2,000 calorie diet.

Easy Slow Cooker Pulled Pork Sandwiches

Ingredients

- 1 1/2 C. barbeque sauce, or more as desired
- 1/2 C. chopped white onion
- 1/4 C. ketchup
- 1/4 C. brown sugar
- 1 tsp salt
- 1 tsp ground black pepper
- 1/2 tsp chili powder
- 1 lb boneless pork loin, quartered
- 4 onion rolls, halved

Directions

- Add the following to the crock of a slow cooker: chili powder, bbq sauce, black pepper, onion, salt, brown sugar, and ketchup.
- Stir the mix until it is smooth then add in the pork and stir everything again.
- Place a lid on the slow cooker and let everything cook for 5 hrs with high heat.
- Now remove the meat and shred it into pieces.
- Then add it back to the crock pot and cook everything for 15 more mins with a low heat.
- Liberally top the bottom half of your onion rolls with the pork then top the meat with the drippings.
- Enjoy.

Amount per serving (4 total)

Timing Information:

Preparation	Cooking	Total Time
10 m	4 h 30 m	4 h 40 m

Nutritional Information:

Calories	504 kcal
Fat	9 g
Carbohydrates	78.6g
Protein	25.7 g
Cholesterol	53 mg
Sodium	2089 mg

* Percent Daily Values are based on a 2,000 calorie diet.

The Tropical Sandwich

Ingredients

- 1/4 C. mango chutney, see appendix
- 4 slices crusty bread, cut diagonally from a large loaf
- 6 slices black forest ham
- 4 slices white Cheddar cheese
- 2 tbsps butter, softened

Directions

- Get a frying pan hot with nonstick spray.
- Layer the following on two pieces of bread: mango chutney, 3 pieces of ham, 2 pieces of cheddar, and remaining pieces of bread.
- Coat the sandwich with butter on all sides.
- Fry for 4 mins per side.
- Enjoy.

Amount per serving (2 total)

Timing Information:

Preparation	Cooking	Total Time
5 mins	5 mins	10 mins

Nutritional Information:

Calories	523 kcal
Fat	34.9 g
Carbohydrates	35.9g
Protein	17.9 g
Cholesterol	90 mg
Sodium	990 mg

* Percent Daily Values are based on a 2,000 calorie diet.

Parmigiano-Reggiano Sandwich

Ingredients

- 1/4 C. butter, softened
- 1 C. freshly grated Parmigiano-Reggiano cheese
- 8 slices cooked bacon
- 4 slices Cheddar cheese
- 8 slices sourdough bread

Directions

- Get a bowl, evenly mix: parmesan, and butter.
- Get a frying hot with nonstick spray.
- Layer one piece of cheddar, and two pieces of bacon on half of your pieces of bread. Then put another piece of bread to form a sandwich. Coat sandwich with butter parmesan mix on both sides.
- Cook for 4 mins per side.
- Enjoy.

Amount per serving (4 total)

Timing Information:

Preparation	Cooking	Total Time
10 mins	6 mins	16 mins

Nutritional Information:

Calories	748 kcal
Fat	50.1 g
Carbohydrates	30.4g
Protein	43 g
Cholesterol	135 mg
Sodium	2211 mg

* Percent Daily Values are based on a 2,000 calorie diet.

Chapter 3: Hot Dogs

Windy City Chicago Hot Dogs

Ingredients

- 4 natural casing beef frankfurters
- 4 hot dog buns
- 1 small onion, diced fine
- 3 -4 tsp sweet pickle relish
- 1 cold-pack kosher dill pickle, quartered lengthwise
- 1 small tomatoes, sliced into julienne strips
- 4 -8 pickled sport bell peppers
- brown mustard, with horseradish, to taste
- celery seed
- poppy seed
- water, for simmering

Directions

- In a pan, add water and frankfurters and simmer for about 10 minutes.
- In a microwave safe plate, place the buns and microwave till slightly warm and soft.
- Arrange 1 frankfurter in each bun and top with the mustard, followed by dill spear, relish, onion, tomato and 1-2 sport peppers.
- Serve with a sprinkling of the celery and poppy seeds.

Amount per serving: 4

Timing Information:

Preparation	15 mins
Total Time	25 mins

Nutritional Information:

Calories	298.9
Fat	14.6g
Cholesterol	22.5mg
Sodium	888.1mg
Carbohydrates	31.8g
Protein	10.8g

* Percent Daily Values are based on a 2,000 calorie diet.

American Picnic Hot Dogs

Ingredients

- 2 hot dogs
- 4 slices bread
- 2 slices American cheese
- ketchup, to taste
- other condiments, to taste

Directions

- Prepare the hot dogs according to package's
- Directions.
- Meanwhile in a toaster, toast the bread.
- Spread the ketchup over the 2 pieced of the bread evenly.
- Arrange 1 cheese slice over the over remaining bread slices.
- Now, slice them down the center lengthwise, and then again horizontally.
- Arrange the hot dog on the bread slices with the cheese.
- Add the condiments of your choice.
- Top with the slices of bread with ketchup.

Amount per serving: 2

Timing Information:

Preparation	15 mins
Total Time	30 mins

Nutritional Information:

Calories	328.5
Fat	18.4g
Cholesterol	32.9mg
Sodium	905.6mg
Carbohydrates	28.3g
Protein	11.6g

* Percent Daily Values are based on a 2,000 calorie diet.

The Simplest Hot Dogs

Ingredients

- 8 hot dogs
- 28 oz. sauerkraut

Directions

- In a large skillet place the sauerkraut and top with the hot dogs.
- Simmer, covered for about 15-20 minutes.
- Serve over the mashed potatoes.

Amount per serving: 4

Timing Information:

Preparation	20 mins
Total Time	20 mins

Nutritional Information:

Calories	336.6
Fat	26.9g
Cholesterol	47.7mg
Sodium	2405.7mg
Carbohydrates	12.5g
Protein	12.0g

* Percent Daily Values are based on a 2,000 calorie diet.

Austrian Style Hot Dogs

Ingredients

- 6 slices turkey bacon
- 1 large onion, sliced and separated into rings
- 4 large hot dogs
- 1 loaf rye bread, sliced in half lengthwise
- 4 slices Swiss cheese
- 2 slices American cheese

Directions

- Heat a large skillet on medium-high heat and cook the bacon till crisp.
- Transfer the bacon onto a paper towel lined plate to drain.
- Drain the grease from the skillet, reserving 2 tbsp in the skillet.
- Add the onion and sauté till tender.
- In a pan of boiling water, cool the hot dogs for about 5 minutes.
- Drain well.
- Set the broiler of your oven.
- Cook the bread under the broiler till toasted.
- Cut the hot dogs in half lengthwise, cutting to but not through the other side.
- Arrange the cut side down of the hot dogs on bottom half of the bread.
- Top with the bacon, followed by the cheese and cooked onions and cook under the broiler for about 1 minute.
- Top with remaining half of the bread.
- Slice into 4 equal sized pieces and serve.

Amount per serving: 4

Timing Information:

Preparation	10 mins
Total Time	30 mins

Nutritional Information:

Calories	710.2
Fat	42.2g
Cholesterol	79.5mg
Sodium	1587.4mg
Carbohydrates	54.6g
Protein	27.1g

* Percent Daily Values are based on a 2,000 calorie diet.

Manhattan Island Hot Dog Topping

Ingredients

- 1 tsp cumin
- 1 C. water
- 1 tsp chili powder
- 1/2 tsp garlic powder
- 1 tbsp sugar
- 1/4 C. ketchup
- 1 tsp dried onion flakes
- 1 dash salt
- 1 lb hamburger

Directions

- In a pan, add all the
- Ingredients and cook for about 10-15 minutes.
- Serve with the yellow mustard and onions.

Amount per serving: 6

Timing Information:

Preparation	5 mins
Total Time	15 mins

Nutritional Information:

Calories	166.2
Fat	8.8g
Cholesterol	50.7mg
Sodium	196.7mg
Carbohydrates	5.3g
Protein	15.9g

* Percent Daily Values are based on a 2,000 calorie diet.

MINNESOTA STYLE HOT DOGS

Ingredients

- 1 C. cornmeal
- 1 3/4 C. flour
- 2 tsp baking powder
- 2 tsp salt
- 1 egg
- 1/3 C. sugar
- milk
- 24 hot dogs
- 24 wooden skewers
- oil

Directions

- In a large bowl, add the cornmeal, flour, baking powder, salt, egg and sugar and mix till well combined.
- Add the milk and mix till a mixture of pancake consistency forms.
- With the paper towels, pat dry the hot dogs.
- Thread the hot dogs onto floured skewers and then coat with the cornmeal mixture evenly.
- In a deep skillet, heat about 2-inch deep oil to 370 degrees F and fry the hot dog skewers for about 2 1/2 minutes.
- Transfer the hot dog skewers onto a paper towel lined plate to drain.
- Drop the remaining cornmeal mixture into the oil and fry till golden brown.
- Transfer the dumplings onto a paper towel lined plate to drain.
- Serve the hot dog skewers alongside the ketchup and mustard tartar sauce.

Amount per serving: 24

Timing Information:

Preparation	10 mins
Total Time	20 mins

Nutritional Information:

Calories	213.9
Fat	13.7g
Cholesterol	31.6mg
Sodium	741.9mg
Carbohydrates	15.5g
Protein	6.6g

* Percent Daily Values are based on a 2,000 calorie diet.

How to Make An American Hot Dog

Ingredients

- 8 hot dogs, sliced down the middle, but not all the way through
- 8 buns, soft and fresh from the bakery
- 1 onion, chopped or sliced in rings
- oil
- butter, to spread on buns

Directions

- In a non-stick pan, heat the oil on medium heat and sauté the onion till browned.
- Transfer the onion into a bowl and cover with a piece of foil to keep warm.
- In the same pan, place the hot dogs, cut side down and cook till browned from both sides.
- Transfer the hot dog into a bowl.
- Split open the buns and spread the butter on them.
- In the same pan, place the buttered buns, face down on medium heat and toast till nicely browned.
- Transfer the toasted buns onto a plate.
- Arrange the hot dog and cooked onions over the bun.
- Top with the mustard and ketchup and serve.

Amount per serving: 4

Timing Information:

Preparation	5 mins
Total Time	15 mins

Nutritional Information:

Calories	547.9
Fat	30.3g
Cholesterol	47.7mg
Sodium	1439.0mg
Carbohydrates	48.7g
Protein	18.5g

* Percent Daily Values are based on a 2,000 calorie diet.

Summer Backyard Hot Dogs

Ingredients

- 1 lb ground beef
- 3/4 C. hot water
- 1 1/2 C. minced onions
- 4 tbsp ballpark mustard
- 3 tsp sugar
- 2 tsp apple cider vinegar
- 2 tsp chili powder
- 1 C. ketchup
- salt
- 4 hot dog buns
- 4 hot dogs

Directions

- Heat a 4 quart pan and cook the ground beef till browned lightly.
- Add the onions and cook for about 5 minutes.
- Stir in the hot water, mustard, sugar, vinegar, chili powder and ketchup and simmer on low heat for about 1 hour, stirring occasionally.
- Stir in the salt.
- Spread the garlic butter over the lightly toasted buns and top with the hot dogs and beef mixture.

Amount per serving: 4

Timing Information:

Preparation	15 mins
Total Time	1 hr 45 mins

Nutritional Information:

Calories	1111.4
Fat	62.5g
Cholesterol	100.9mg
Sodium	9965.5mg4
Carbohydrates	87.4g
Protein	64.7g

* Percent Daily Values are based on a 2,000 calorie diet.

Brooklyn Style Hot Dogs

Ingredients

- 2 dill pickles, chopped
- 1 (4 oz.) cans diced green chilies
- 2 tbsp onions, chopped
- 2 tbsp yellow mustard
- 8 hot dogs, your favorite brand
- 8 hot dog buns

Directions

- Set your grill and lightly, grease the grill grate.
- In a bowl, mix together the pickles, chilies, onion and mustard.
- Cook the hot dogs on the grill till desired doneness.
- Arrange the hot dogs over the bun and top with the pickle mixture.

Amount per serving: 8

Timing Information:

Preparation	5 mins
Total Time	15 mins

Nutritional Information:

Calories	276.9
Fat	15.3g
Cholesterol	23.8mg
Sodium	1071.3mg
Carbohydrates	24.6g
Protein	9.5g

* Percent Daily Values are based on a 2,000 calorie diet.

Gourmet Hot Dogs

Ingredients

- 8 hot dog buns
- mayonnaise
- sweet relish
- mustard
- 8 beef hot dogs
- 1 (16 oz.) cans chili
- cheddar cheese, shredded
- 1/2 onion, chopped

Directions

- Set your oven to 350 degrees F before doing anything else and line a 13x9-inch baking dish with a piece of foil.
- Coat the inside of the hot dog buns with the mayonnaise and sweet relish and top with the mustard evenly.
- In the prepared baking dish, arrange the hot dogs, side-by-side and top with the chili, cheese and diced onion.
- With a piece of the foil, cover the baking dish.
- Cook in the oven for about 45 minutes.

Amount per serving: 1

Timing Information:

| Preparation | 10 mins |
| Total Time | 55 mins |

Nutritional Information:

Calories	335.2
Fat	18.3g
Cholesterol	33.5mg
Sodium	1017.5mg
Carbohydrates	30.5g
Protein	12.4g

* Percent Daily Values are based on a 2,000 calorie diet.

Chapter 4: French Fries

Georgia Backroad Fries

Ingredients

- 1 1/2 cups all-purpose flour
- 1 1/2 teaspoons paprika
- 1 teaspoon salt
- 1/2 teaspoon ground black pepper
- 1/2 teaspoon chili powder
- 1/4 teaspoon cayenne pepper
- 1 egg
- 1/3 cup milk
- 6 potatoes, cut into wedges
- 1/4 cup vegetable oil

Directions

- Coat a jelly roll pan with oil then set your oven to 450 degrees before doing anything else.
- Get bowl, combine: cayenne, flour, chili powder, paprika, black pepper, and salt.
- Get a 2nd bowl, combine: milk and eggs. Whisk everything together evenly. Then evenly coat your potatoes with the egg mix then the dry mix.
- Place everything on the jelly roll pan then top the wedges with the veggie oil evenly.
- Cook everything in the oven for about 22 to 26 mins.
- Enjoy.

Amount per serving 6

Timing Information:

Preparation	15 m
Cooking	20 m
Total Time	35 m

Nutritional Information:

Calories	10.8 g
Fat	62.4g
Carbohydrates	9.2 g
Protein	32 mg
Cholesterol	421 mg
Sodium	10.8 g

* Percent Daily Values are based on a 2,000 calorie diet.

New Jersey Diner Style Fries

Ingredients

- 1 large baking potato, cut into wedges
- 1 tablespoon olive oil
- 1/2 teaspoon paprika
- 1/2 tsp Italian seasoning
- 1/2 teaspoon garlic powder
- 1/2 teaspoon chili powder
- 1/2 teaspoon onion powder

Directions

- Set your oven to 450 degrees before doing anything else.
- Get a bowl for your potatoes and combine with them: onion powder, olive oil, chili powder, garlic powder, Italian spice, and paprika.
- Lay our wedges on a baking sheet that has been coated with non-stick spray then cook everything in the oven for 40 to 46 mins.
- Enjoy.

Amount per serving 1

Timing Information:

Preparation	5 m
Cooking	45 m
Total Time	50 m

Nutritional Information:

Calories	357 kcal
Fat	14.1 g
Carbohydrates	54.7g
Protein	5.4 g
Cholesterol	0 mg
Sodium	27 mg

* Percent Daily Values are based on a 2,000 calorie diet.

French Fry Dinner Bake

Ingredients

- 1 tablespoon vegetable oil
- 1 1/2 pounds lean ground beef
- 1/2 onion, diced
- 1/2 green bell pepper, diced
- salt and black pepper to taste
- 1 10.75 ounce can condensed cream of mushroom soup
- 3/4 cup processed cheese sauce such as Cheez Whiz
- 1/2 28 ounce package frozen shoestring potato fries

Directions

- Coat a casserole dish with oil then set your oven to 400 degrees before doing anything else.
- As the oven heats begin to fry your ground beef in oil then combine in the green pepper and onion. Stir fry the beef for 14 mins until it is fully done. Add some pepper and salt then combine in the soup. Stir everything together, then get the mix simmering. Once everything is gently boiling, set the heat to low.
- Place your cheese in the microwave for about 45 secs to melt down then layer the beef into the casserole dish. Top the beef with the cheese then layer your fries over everything.
- Cook the dish in the oven for 20 mins or until everything the fries are finished.
- Enjoy.

Amount per serving 6

Timing Information:

Preparation	10 m
Cooking	40 m
Total Time	50 m

Nutritional Information:

Calories	476 kcal
Fat	29 g
Carbohydrates	24.9g
Protein	28 g
Cholesterol	99 mg
Sodium	31214 mg

* Percent Daily Values are based on a 2,000 calorie diet.

SIMPLE PORTUGUESE INSPIRED FRIES

Ingredients

- 1 quart oil for frying
- 3 large potatoes, julienned
- 3 cups chopped fresh cilantro
- salt and pepper to taste

Directions

- Get your oil hot to about 350 degrees in a Dutch oven.
- Working in batches cook about one third of the potatoes in the oil for about 6 mins. Then add in the cilantro and continue cooking them for 60 more secs. Place the potatoes to the side on some paper towel lined plates.
- Continue frying potatoes in batches like this and draining them. After all the potatoes have been fried and drain top them with some pepper and salt.
- Enjoy.

Amount per serving 6

Timing Information:

Preparation	30 m
Cooking	30 m
Total Time	1 h

Nutritional Information:

Calories	277 kcal
Fat	15 g
Carbohydrates	33.1g
Protein	4.2 g
Cholesterol	0 mg
Sodium	409 mg

* Percent Daily Values are based on a 2,000 calorie diet.

Elegant Truffle Oil and Parsley Fries

Ingredients

- cooking spray
- 1 pound potatoes, cut into strips - or more to taste
- salt and ground black pepper to taste
- 1 tablespoon white truffle oil, or to taste
- 2 teaspoons chopped fresh parsley, or more to taste

Directions

- Coat a jelly roll pan with non-stick spray then set your oven to 350 degrees before doing anything else.
- Layer your potato on the jelly roll pan and top them with a bit nonstick spray. Toss the potatoes then top them with some pepper and salt and toss everything again.
- Cook the potatoes in the oven for 35 mins then let them loose their heat. Place everything into a bowl and coat the potatoes evenly with more salt, parsley, and truffle oil. Stir the potatoes to evenly coat them with oil and spice.
- Enjoy.

Amount per serving 4

Timing Information:

Preparation	15 m
Cooking	30 m
Total Time	50 m

Nutritional Information:

Calories	120 kcal
Fat	3.7 g
Carbohydrates	19.9g
Protein	2.3 g
Cholesterol	0 mg
Sodium	7 mg

* Percent Daily Values are based on a 2,000 calorie diet.

Seasoned Crinkle Cuts

Ingredients

- 5 cups frozen crinkle cut French fries
- 1 teaspoon onion salt
- 1/4 teaspoon paprika
- 1/3 cup grated parmesan cheese

Directions

- Set your oven to 450 degrees before doing anything else.
- Get a casserole dish and coat it with nonstick spray. Place your fries in the dish and top them with the paprika and onion salt.
- Toss everything evenly to coat the fries nicely.
- Cook your fries in the oven for about 17 mins to 22 mins or until completely done. Once the fries are finished top them with the parmesan cheese.
- Enjoy.

Amount per serving: 4

Timing Information:

Preparation	5 mins
Total Time	20 mins

Nutritional Information:

Calories	36.2
Fat	2.4g
Cholesterol	7.3mg
Sodium	127.3mg
Carbohydrates	0.4g
Protein	3.2g

* Percent Daily Values are based on a 2,000 calorie diet.

How to Bake French Fries

Ingredients

- cooking spray
- 2 large potatoes, cut into 1/4-inch slices
- 2 tablespoons vegetable oil
- 1/4 cup grated Parmesan cheese
- 1 tablespoon garlic powder
- 1 tablespoon chopped fresh basil
- 1 tablespoon salt
- 1 tablespoon coarsely ground black pepper

Directions

- Set your oven to 375 degrees before doing anything else.
- Get a casserole dish and cover it with foil. Coat the foil with some nonstick spray then place your potatoes in a bowl.
- Cover your potatoes with veggie oil and toss them then combine in the black pepper, parmesan, salt, basil, and garlic powder. Toss everything again to evenly coat the potatoes then layer them into the casserole dish evenly.
- Cook everything in the oven for 31 to 36 mins or until the fries are golden.
- Enjoy.

Amount per serving 4

Timing Information:

Preparation	10 m
Cooking	30 m
Total Time	40 m

Nutritional Information:

Calories	236 kcal
Fat	8.5 g
Carbohydrates	35g
Protein	6.2 g
Cholesterol	4 mg
Sodium	1833 mg

* Percent Daily Values are based on a 2,000 calorie diet.

Louisiana Creole Fries

Ingredients

- 1/4 cup olive oil
- 1 teaspoon garlic powder
- 1 teaspoon onion powder
- 1 teaspoon chili powder
- 1 teaspoon Cajun/Creole seasoning, see appendix
- 1 teaspoon sea salt
- 6 large baking potatoes, sliced into thin wedges

Directions

- Set your oven to 400 degrees before doing anything else.
- Get a bowl, combine: sea salt, olive oil, Cajun/creole spice, garlic powder, chili powder, and onion powder. Stir the spice together evenly then combine in the potatoes.
- Toss everything together evenly then layer it all in a casserole dish spaced out evenly.
- Cook the fries in the oven for about 30 to 37 mins then flip the potatoes and continue bake them for 8 more mins.
- Enjoy.

Amount per serving 6

Timing Information:

Preparation	15 m
Cooking	45 m
Total Time	1 h

Nutritional Information:

Calories	369 kcal
Fat	9.4 g
Carbohydrates	65.5g
Protein	7.7 g
Cholesterol	0 mg
Sodium	399 mg

* Percent Daily Values are based on a 2,000 calorie diet

Easy Aztec Style Fries

Ingredients

- 2 pounds yucca, peeled, and cut into 4 inch sections
- 2 quarts vegetable oil for frying
- salt to taste

Directions

- Get your yucca boiling in a saucepan. Once the mix is boiling place a lid on the pot, set the heat to low and let gently boil for 25 mins. Remove the liquid then slice the yucca into matchsticks when they have cool off enough to be handled easily.
- Remember to discard the hard inner center of the yuccas.
- Begin to get your oil hot to about 350 to 370 degrees then once the oil is hot working in sets fry about 1/3 to 1/4 of the fries for about 6 to 7 mins per set.
- Lay your yucca fries out to drain then once everything is cool top them with salt.
- Enjoy.

Amount per serving 6

Timing Information:

Preparation	15 m
Cooking	35 m
Total Time	1 h

Nutritional Information:

Calories	437 kcal
Fat	29.3 g
Carbohydrates	40.9g
Protein	5.3 g
Cholesterol	0 mg
Sodium	73 mg

* Percent Daily Values are based on a 2,000 calorie diet.

Indian Style Curry Cumin Fries

Ingredients

- 1 russet potato, cut into evenly sized strips
- 1 quart vegetable oil for frying
- 1/4 tsp curry powder
- 1/4 tsp cumin
- salt to taste

Directions

- Let your potato sit submerged in water for 45 mins. Then drain and dry them evenly.
- Get your oil hot in a Dutch oven to about 270 to 275 degrees then fry the potatoes for 6 mins in the hot oil for 2 mins then flip the fries and fry them for about 2 to 3 mins. Place the fries on a paper towel lined plate to drain and continue frying everything in batches.
- Once all the fries have been cooked increase the temperature of the oil to 350 degrees and working in batched re-fry your potatoes for 4 to 5 mins then place them to the side again to drain.
- Place all the fries into a bowl then top them with cumin, curry, and salt and toss everything completely and evenly.
- Enjoy.

Amount per serving 2

Timing Information:

Preparation	10 m
Cooking	10 m
Total Time	50 m

Nutritional Information:

Calories	437 kcal
Fat	29.3 g
Carbohydrates	40.9g
Protein	5.3 g
Cholesterol	0 mg
Sodium	73 mg

* Percent Daily Values are based on a 2,000 calorie diet.

Chapter 5: Coleslaw

6 Ingredient Coleslaw

Ingredients

- 2 C. mayonnaise
- 1 C. buttermilk
- 3 tbsp white sugar
- 1 tsp celery seed
- 1/2 tsp ground black pepper
- 2 (16 oz.) packages shredded coleslaw mix

Directions

- In a large bowl, add the mayonnaise, buttermilk, sugar, celery seed and black pepper and mix well.
- Fold in the coleslaw mix and refrigerate to chill before serving.

Amount per serving (12 total)

Timing Information:

Preparation	
Cooking	10 m
Total Time	40 m

Nutritional Information:

Calories	343 kcal
Fat	31.3 g
Carbohydrates	14.7g
Protein	2 g
Cholesterol	21 mg
Sodium	247 mg

* Percent Daily Values are based on a 2,000 calorie diet.

Dijon Raisin Coleslaw

Ingredients

- 1 red onion, thinly sliced
- 1 red bell pepper, thinly sliced
- 3 C. shredded cabbage
- 1 large carrot, shredded
- 1/2 C. raisins
- 1/4 C. mayonnaise
- 1/2 C. sour cream
- 2 tbsp Dijon-style prepared mustard
- 1 tsp white wine vinegar

Directions

- In a large bowl, mix together the onion, red pepper, cabbage, carrot and raisins.
- In a small bowl, add the mayonnaise, sour cream, mustard and vinegar and beat till well combined.
- Place the dressing over vegetable mixture and toss to coat well.
- Refrigerate for at least 2 hours before serving.

Amount per serving (7 total)

Timing Information:

Preparation	
Cooking	15 m
Total Time	1 h 15 m

Nutritional Information:

Calories	150 kcal
Fat	9.9 g
Carbohydrates	15.3g
Protein	1.7 g
Cholesterol	10 mg
Sodium	175 mg

* Percent Daily Values are based on a 2,000 calorie diet.

Mexican Style Coleslaw

Ingredients

- 1/2 (16 oz.) package shredded coleslaw mix
- 1/2 tsp seasoning salt
- 1 tbsp lemon juice
- 2 tbsp olive oil
- 1/2 C. mayonnaise
- 1/2 C. salsa

Directions

- In a large bowl, add the coleslaw, seasoning salt, lemon juice, olive oil, mayonnaise and salsa and toss till well combined.
- Serve immediately.

Amount per serving (3 total)

Timing Information:

Preparation	
Cooking	10 m
Total Time	10 m

Nutritional Information:

Calories	415 kcal
Fat	40.1 g
Carbohydrates	13.7g
Protein	2 g
Cholesterol	20 mg
Sodium	638 mg

* Percent Daily Values are based on a 2,000 calorie diet.

Coleslaw Crossroads

Ingredients

- 1 medium head cabbage, shredded
- 1 large red onion, diced
- 1 C. grated carrots
- 2 stalks celery, chopped
- 1 C. white sugar
- 1 C. white vinegar
- 3/4 C. vegetable oil
- 1 tbsp salt
- 1 tbsp dry mustard
- black pepper to taste

Directions

- In a large bowl, mix together the cabbage, onion, carrots and celery.
- Sprinkle with 1 C. of the sugar and mix well.
- In a small pan, mix together the vinegar, oil, salt, dry mustard and pepper and bring to a boil.
- Place the hot dressing over the cabbage mixture and mix well.

Amount per serving (20 total)

Timing Information:

Preparation	
Cooking	30 m
Total Time	30 m

Nutritional Information:

Calories	131 kcal
Fat	8.4 g
Carbohydrates	14.1g
Protein	0.9 g
Cholesterol	0 mg
Sodium	364 mg

* Percent Daily Values are based on a 2,000 calorie diet.

San Antonio Coleslaw

Ingredients

- 1 C. mayonnaise
- 1 tbsp lime juice
- 1 tbsp ground cumin
- 1 tsp cayenne pepper
- 1 tsp salt
- 1 tsp ground black pepper
- 1 medium head green cabbage, rinsed and very thinly sliced
- 1 large carrot, shredded
- 2 green onions, sliced
- 2 radishes, sliced

Directions

- In a large bowl, add the mayonnaise, lime juice, cumin, salt and pepper and beat till well combined.
- Add the cabbage, carrot, green onions and radishes and mix till well combined
- Refrigerate to chill for at least 1 hour before serving.

Amount per serving (8 total)

Timing Information:

Preparation	
Cooking	15 m
Total Time	1 h 15 m

Nutritional Information:

Calories	236 kcal
Fat	22.2 g
Carbohydrates	9.4g
Protein	2.1 g
Cholesterol	10 mg
Sodium	476 mg

* Percent Daily Values are based on a 2,000 calorie diet.

Buttermilk Coleslaw

Ingredients

- 1 (16 oz.) package coleslaw mix
- 2 tbsp minced onion
- 1/3 C. white sugar
- 1/2 tsp salt
- 1/8 tsp ground black pepper
- 1/4 C. milk
- 1/2 C. mayonnaise
- 1/4 C. buttermilk
- 1 1/2 tbsp white wine vinegar
- 2 1/2 tbsp lemon juice

Directions

- In a large bowl, mix together the coleslaw and onion.
- In another bowl, add the sugar, salt, pepper, milk, mayonnaise, buttermilk, vinegar and lemon juice and mix till smooth.
- Place the dressing over the coleslaw and onion and mix well.
- Refrigerate to chill for at least 1 hour before serving.

Amount per serving (8 total)

Timing Information:

Preparation	
Cooking	15 m
Total Time	1 h 15 m

Nutritional Information:

Calories	184 kcal
Fat	12.6 g
Carbohydrates	17.1g
Protein	1.4 g
Cholesterol	11 mg
Sodium	248 mg

* Percent Daily Values are based on a 2,000 calorie diet.

Autumn Picnic Coleslaw

Ingredients

- 1 C. mayonnaise
- 2 tbsp sugar
- 1/2 tsp salt
- 1/2 tsp pepper
- 1/2 tsp celery seed
- 1/2 tsp garlic powder
- 1/2 tsp onion powder
- 2 tbsp cider vinegar
- 1 (16 oz.) package shredded coleslaw mix

Directions

- In a large bowl, add the mayonnaise, sugar, salt, pepper, celery seed, garlic powder, onion powder and cider vinegar and mix well.
- Add the coleslaw mix and toss to coat.
- Refrigerate to chill for at least 1 hour before serving.

Amount per serving (8 total)

Timing Information:

Preparation	
Cooking	10 m
Total Time	1 h 10 m

Nutritional Information:

Calories	256 kcal
Fat	23.3 g
Carbohydrates	11.4g
Protein	1.1 g
Cholesterol	15 mg
Sodium	315 mg

* Percent Daily Values are based on a 2,000 calorie diet.

Hawaiian Coleslaw

Ingredients

- 3 tbsp creamy peanut butter
- 2 cloves garlic, minced
- 1/2 tsp salt
- 2 tbsp rice vinegar
- 2 tbsp soy sauce
- 1/8 tsp hot pepper sauce (e.g. Tabasco(TM))
- 1/2 C. chopped cilantro leaves
- 2 tbsp chopped fresh chives
- 2 red bell peppers, thinly sliced
- 8 C. shredded cabbage
- 2 tbsp toasted sesame seeds (optional)

Directions

- In a large bowl, add the peanut butter, garlic, salt, rice vinegar, soy sauce and hot pepper sauce and mix till smooth.
- Add the cilantro, chives, red pepper and shredded cabbage and mix well. S
- With a plastic wrap, cover the bowl and refrigerate for about 1 hour.
- Serve with a sprinkling of the sesame seeds.

Amount per serving (8 total)

Timing Information:

Preparation	
Cooking	40 m
Total Time	1 h 40 m

Nutritional Information:

Calories	80 kcal
Fat	4.4 g
Carbohydrates	8.3g
Protein	3.5 g
Cholesterol	0 mg
Sodium	415 mg

* Percent Daily Values are based on a 2,000 calorie diet.

Apple Cider Grapeseed Coleslaw

Ingredients

- 1 medium head green cabbage, finely shredded
- 3 tbsp finely chopped garlic
- 1 1/2 tsp kosher salt
- 1/3 C. grapeseed oil
- 1/3 C. mayonnaise
- 1/3 C. apple cider vinegar
- 1/4 tsp ground paprika
- 1/4 tsp ground white pepper
- 1/8 tsp white sugar
- 1/8 tsp celery seed

Directions

- In a large bowl, place the shredded cabbage.
- Place the chopped garlic into a mound on a cutting board and sprinkle with the salt.
- With the flat side of a chef's knife, smash the garlic and salt together and transfer into a bowl.
- Add the grapeseed oil, mayonnaise, apple cider vinegar, ground paprika, ground white pepper, sugar and celery seed in the bowl with the garlic mixture and beat till smooth.
- Place the dressing over the shredded cabbage and toss to coat well.
- With the back of a spoon, press the coleslaw down in the bowl and refrigerate, covered for at least 1 hour.
- Stir well before serving.

Amount per serving (8 total)

Timing Information:

Preparation	
Cooking	15 m
Total Time	1 h 15 m

Nutritional Information:

Calories	182 kcal
Fat	16.5 g
Carbohydrates	8.2g
Protein	1.8 g
Cholesterol	3 mg
Sodium	434 mg

* Percent Daily Values are based on a 2,000 calorie diet.

Garden Fresh Coleslaw

Ingredients

- 2 C. shredded zucchini
- 1 C. shredded carrot
- 1/4 C. low-fat creamy salad dressing (such as Miracle Whip Light(R))
- 1 tsp white sugar
- salt and ground black pepper to taste

Directions

- In a colander, add the zucchini and keep aside for about 30 minutes to drain completely.
- In a large salad bowl, mix together the zucchini and carrot.
- Add the creamy salad dressing and sugar and stir to combine.
- Refrigerate to chill for about 1 hour.
- Season with the salt and black pepper and stir again.

Amount per serving (8 total)

Timing Information:

Preparation	
Cooking	15 m
Total Time	1 h 45 m

Nutritional Information:

Calories	31 kcal
Fat	1.6 g
Carbohydrates	4g
Protein	0.6 g
Cholesterol	2 mg
Sodium	< 126 mg

* Percent Daily Values are based on a 2,000 calorie diet.

Chapter 6: Fried Chicken

Crispy Garlicky Fried Chicken

Ingredients

- 2 tsp garlic powder
- 1 tsp ground black pepper
- 1 tsp salt
- 1 tsp paprika
- 1/2 C. seasoned bread crumbs
- 1 C. all-purpose flour
- 1/2 C. milk
- 1 egg
- 4 skinless, boneless chicken breast halves
- 1 C. oil for frying, or as needed

Directions

- In a shallow dish, add the egg and milk and beat well.
- In another shallow dish mix together the flour, breadcrumbs, garlic powder, paprika, salt and black pepper.
- Get your oil, in a skillet to 350 degrees F.
- Dip the chicken breast halves in the egg mixture and then roll in the flour mixture evenly.
- Fry the chicken breast halves for about 10 minutes, flipping once half way.
- Serve hot.

Amount per serving (4 total)

Timing Information:

Preparation	20 m
Cooking	15 m
Total Time	35 m

Nutritional Information:

Calories	391 kcal
Fat	11.4 g
Carbohydrates	37.3g
Protein	32.8 g
Cholesterol	116 mg
Sodium	935 mg

* Percent Daily Values are based on a 2,000 calorie diet.

Cheesy Parsley Parmesan Oven Fried Chicken

Ingredients

- 1 clove crushed garlic
- 1/4 lb. butter, melted
- 1 C. dried bread crumbs
- 1/3 C. grated Parmesan cheese
- 2 tbsp chopped fresh parsley
- 1 tsp salt
- 1/8 tsp ground black pepper
- 1 (4 lb.) chicken, cut into pieces

Directions

- Set your oven to 350 degrees F before doing anything else and grease a 13x9-inch baking dish.
- In a shallow dish, mix together the melted butter and garlic.
- In another shallow dish, mix together the cheese, breadcrumbs, parsley, salt and black pepper.
- Coat the chicken pieces in the butter mixture and in the cheese mixture evenly.
- Arrange the chicken pieces into the prepared baking dish in a single layer.
- Drizzle with the remaining butter mixture evenly and cook everything in the oven for about 1-1 1/4 hours.

Amount per serving (6 total)

Timing Information:

Preparation	15 m
Cooking	1 h 15 m
Total Time	1 h 30 m

Nutritional Information:

Calories	607 kcal
Fat	40.4 g
Carbohydrates	13.4g
Protein	45.1 g
Cholesterol	174 mg
Sodium	821 mg

* Percent Daily Values are based on a 2,000 calorie diet.

Buttermilk Paprika Fried Chicken

Ingredients

- 1 (4 lb.) chicken, cut into pieces
- 1 C. buttermilk
- 2 C. all-purpose flour for coating
- 1 tsp paprika
- salt and pepper to taste
- 2 quarts vegetable oil for frying

Directions

- In a shallow dish, place the buttermilk.
- In another shallow dish, place the flour, salt, black pepper and paprika.
- Dip the chicken pieces in the buttermilk completely and coat them in the flour mixture.
- Arrange the chicken pieces on a baking dish and cover with wax paper and keep aside till flour becomes pasty.
- In a large cast iron skillet, heat the vegetable oil and fry the chicken pieces till browned.
- Reduce the heat and cook, covered for about 30 minutes.
- Uncover and increase the heat and cook till crispy.
- Transfer the chicken pieces onto paper towel lined plates to drain.

Amount per serving (8 total)

Timing Information:

Preparation	30 min
Cooking	20 min
Total Time	50 min

Nutritional Information:

Calories	489 kcal
Fat	21.8 g
Carbohydrates	29.5g
Protein	40.7 g
Cholesterol	116 mg
Sodium	140 mg

* Percent Daily Values are based on a 2,000 calorie diet.

6-Ingredient Fried Chicken

Ingredients

- 1 (3 lb.) whole chicken, cut into pieces
- 1 C. all-purpose flour
- salt to taste
- ground black pepper to taste
- 1 tsp paprika
- 1 quart vegetable oil for frying

Directions

- In a shallow dish, place the flour.
- Sprinkle the chicken pieces with salt, paprika and black pepper and roll them in the flour evenly.
- In a large skillet, heat the oil to 365 degrees F.
- Add the chicken pieces and cook, covered for about 15-20 minutes, flipping once half way.
- Transfer the chicken pieces onto paper towel lined plates to drain.

Amount per serving (6 total)

Timing Information:

Preparation	15 m
Cooking	20 m
Total Time	35 m

Nutritional Information:

Calories	491 kcal
Fat	32 g
Carbohydrates	16.1g
Protein	32.8 g
Cholesterol	97 mg
Sodium	94 mg

* Percent Daily Values are based on a 2,000 calorie diet.

Indian Style Fried Chicken

Ingredients

- 1 (4 lb.) whole chicken, cut into pieces
- 6 cloves garlic, chopped
- 4 tbsp oyster sauce
- 2 tbsp curry powder
- 1/2 C. vegetable oil

Directions

- In a glass dish, mix together the oyster sauce, garlic and curry powder.
- Add the chicken pieces and coat it with the mixture generously.
- Cover and refrigerate for at least 1/2 hour.
- In a large skillet, heat the oil on medium-high heat and fry the chicken pieces for about 20-25 minutes

Amount per serving (4 total)

Timing Information:

Preparation	15 m
Cooking	25 m
Total Time	1 h 15 m

Nutritional Information:

Calories	1238 kcal
Fat	96.3 g
Carbohydrates	13.8g
Protein	85.2 g
Cholesterol	1340 mg
Sodium	1430 mg

* Percent Daily Values are based on a 2,000 calorie diet.

Crispy Fried Chicken Croquettes

Ingredients

- 1/4 C. butter
- 1/4 C. flour
- 1/2 C. milk
- 1/2 C. chicken broth
- 3 C. finely chopped cooked chicken
- 1 1/2 C. seasoned bread crumbs, divided
- 2 eggs, beaten
- 1/4 C. minced onion
- 1 tbsp dried parsley
- 1/4 tsp garlic powder
- 1/8 tsp celery seed
- 1/8 tsp cayenne pepper
- salt and ground black pepper to taste
- 1/4 C. oil, or as needed

Directions

- In a pan, melt the butter on medium heat.
- Slowly, add the flour, stirring continuously and cook for about 1 minute.
- Slowly, add the broth and the milk, beating continuously.
- Cook, stirring continuously for about 5-10 minute till a thick sauce forms.
- Remove everything from the heat and keep aside for about 10 minutes to cool.
- In a large bowl, add the cooled sauce, chicken, eggs, 1 C. of the breadcrumbs, onion, parsley, celery seeds, garlic powder, salt and black pepper and mix till well combined.
- Cover and refrigerate to marinate for about 2 hours.
- Make 6 equal sized patties from the mixture.
- In a shallow, dish place the remaining breadcrumbs.

- Roll the each patty in the breadcrumbs.
- In a large skillet, heat the oil on medium-high heat and cook the patties for about 5 minutes per side.
- Transfer the chicken onto paper towel lined plates to drain.

Amount per serving (6 total)

Timing Information:

Preparation	25 m
Cooking	30 m
Total Time	2 h 55 m

Nutritional Information:

Calories	377 kcal
Fat	17.5 g
Carbohydrates	26.6g
Protein	27 g
Cholesterol	137 mg
Sodium	765 mg

* Percent Daily Values are based on a 2,000 calorie diet.

Oriental Fried Chicken Thighs

Ingredients

- 4 eggs
- 1/4 C. cornstarch
- 1/4 C. white sugar
- 5 cloves garlic, minced
- 1/2 C. sweet rice flour
- 4 tsp salt
- 4 green onions, chopped
- 1/4 C. oyster sauce
- 5 lb. boneless chicken thighs, cut in half
- 2 C. vegetable oil, for deep frying

Directions

- In a large bowl, mix together all the ingredients except the chicken and oil.
- Add the chicken pieces and coat them with the mixture generously.
- Cover and refrigerate everything to marinate overnight.
- Remove the chicken pieces from the refrigerator and keep everything aside in at room temperature for about 10 minutes before cooking.
- In a large skillet, heat the oil to 375 degrees F and fry the chicken pieces till golden brown completely.
- Transfer the chicken pieces onto paper towel lined plates to drain.

Amount per serving (10 total)

Timing Information:

Preparation	10 m
Cooking	40 m
Total Time	8 h 50 m

Nutritional Information:

Calories	877 kcal
Fat	68.5 g
Carbohydrates	120.4g
Protein	44 g
Cholesterol	222 mg
Sodium	1137 mg

* Percent Daily Values are based on a 2,000 calorie diet.

Kanas Style Fried Chicken Cutlets

Ingredients

- 3 C. cold water
- 1/4 C. kosher salt
- 1/4 C. honey
- 4 boneless skinless chicken breast halves
- 1/4 C. buttermilk
- 1 C. all-purpose flour
- 1 tsp black pepper
- 1/2 tsp garlic salt
- 1/2 tsp onion salt
- cayenne pepper to taste
- vegetable oil for frying

Directions

- In a large bowl, add the water, honey and salt and mix till the honey is dissolved. Add the chicken breast halves and coat with the honey mixture generously and place a heavy plate over the chicken to submerge it completely.
- Cover and refrigerate everything to marinate for about 1 hour.
- Remove the chicken breast halves from the marinade and pat it dry with a paper towel and transfer the meat to a bowl.
- Add the buttermilk and keep it aside for about 15 minutes.
- In a shallow dish, place the flour, onion salt, garlic salt, cayenne pepper, salt and black pepper.
- Coat the chicken breast halves with the flour mixture evenly and arrange everything on a wire rack for about 15 minutes.
- In a large skillet, heat the oil to 350 degrees F and fry the chicken breast halves for about 15-20 minutes.
- Transfer the chicken onto paper towel lined plates to drain.

Amount per serving (4 total)

Timing Information:

Preparation	10 m
Cooking	15 m
Total Time	1 h 45 m

Nutritional Information:

Calories	481 kcal
Fat	21.5 g
Carbohydrates	49.4g
Protein	22.8 g
Cholesterol	65 mg
Sodium	6378 mg

* Percent Daily Values are based on a 2,000 calorie diet.

FRIED CHICKEN IN A JAPANESE STYLE

Ingredients

- 2 eggs, lightly beaten
- 1/2 tsp salt
- 1/2 tsp black pepper
- 1/2 tsp white sugar
- 1 tbsp minced garlic
- 1 tbsp grated fresh ginger root
- 1 tbsp sesame oil
- 1 tbsp soy sauce
- 1/8 tsp chicken bouillon granules
- 1 1/2 lb. skinless, boneless chicken breast halves - cut into 1 inch cubes
- 3 tbsp potato starch
- 1 tbsp rice flour
- oil for frying

Directions

- In a large bowl, add the eggs, gingerroot, garlic, soy sauce, sesame oil, bouillon granules, sugar, salt and black pepper and mix well.
- Add the chicken cubes and coat them with the mixture generously and refrigerate, covered for about 30 minutes.
- In a large skillet, heat the oil to 365 degrees F and fry the chicken cubes till golden brown.
- Transfer the chicken onto paper towel lined plates to drain.

Amount per serving (8 total)

Timing Information:

Preparation	20 m
Cooking	20 m
Total Time	1 h 10 m

Nutritional Information:

Calories	256 kcal
Fat	16.7 g
Carbohydrates	4.8g
Protein	20.9 g
Cholesterol	98 mg
Sodium	327 mg

* Percent Daily Values are based on a 2,000 calorie diet.

Fried Chicken with Honey Nut Sauce

Ingredients

- 1 quart peanut oil for frying
- 1 whole chicken, cut into 8 pieces
- 1 tsp seasoned salt
- 2 eggs, beaten
- 2 C. self-rising flour
- 1 pinch salt and ground black pepper
- 1 C. butter
- 1/2 C. honey
- 1 C. chopped pecans

Directions

- Sprinkle the chicken pieces with the seasoned salt evenly.
- In a shallow dish, mix together the flour, salt and black pepper.
- Add the chicken and coat it with the mixture generously.
- In a large skillet, heat the oil to 375 degrees F and fry the chicken pieces for about 10 minutes on both sides.
- Transfer the chicken onto paper towel lined plates to drain.
- In a pan, melt the butter on medium heat and add the honey beating continuously.
- Cook, beating continuously, for about 5 minutes.
- Reduce the heat to low and simmer for about 10 minutes.
- Stir in the pecans and cook for about 2-3 minutes.
- Pour the honey mixture over the chicken and serve.

Amount per serving (8 total)

Timing Information:

Preparation	15 m
Cooking	40 m
Total Time	55 m

Nutritional Information:

Calories	846 kcal
Fat	59.7 g
Carbohydrates	45.8g
Protein	33.6 g
Cholesterol	194 mg
Sodium	774 mg

* Percent Daily Values are based on a 2,000 calorie diet.

Chapter 7: Salads

American Potato Salad

Ingredients

- 5 potatoes
- 3 eggs
- 1 C. diced celery
- 1/2 C. diced onion
- 1/2 C. sweet pickle relish
- 1/4 tsp garlic salt
- 1/4 tsp celery salt
- 1 tbsp prepared mustard
- ground black pepper to taste
- 1/4 C. mayonnaise

Directions

- Boil your potatoes in water and salt for 20 mins. Then remove the skins and chunk them.
- Now get your eggs boiling in water.
- Once the water is boiling, place a lid on the pot, and shut the heat.
- Let the eggs sit for 15 mins. Then once they have cooled remove the shells, and dice them.
- Get a bowl, combine: mayo, potatoes, pepper, eggs, mustard, celery, celery salt, onions, garlic, and relish.
- Place a covering of plastic on the mix and put everything in the fridge until it is cold.
- Enjoy.

Amount per serving (8 total)

Timing Information:

Preparation	45 m
Cooking	15 m
Total Time	1 h

Nutritional Information:

Calories	206 kcal
Fat	7.6 g
Carbohydrates	30.5g
Protein	5.5 g
Cholesterol	72 mg
Sodium	335 mg

* Percent Daily Values are based on a 2,000 calorie diet.

Egg Salad

Ingredients

- 8 eggs
- 1/2 C. mayonnaise
- 1 tsp prepared yellow mustard
- 1/4 C. diced green onion
- salt and pepper to taste
- 1/4 tsp paprika

Directions

- Boil your eggs in water for 2 mins then place a lid on the pot and let the contents sit for 15 mins. Once the eggs have cooled remove their shells and dice them.
- Now get a bowl, combine: green onions, eggs, mustard, and mayo.
- Stir the mix until it is smooth then add in the paprika, pepper, and salt.
- Stir the contents again then enjoy with toasted buns.

Amount per serving (4 total)

Timing Information:

Preparation	10 m
Cooking	15 m
Total Time	35 m

Nutritional Information:

Calories	344 kcal
Fat	31.9 g
Carbohydrates	2.3g
Protein	< 13 g
Cholesterol	382 mg
Sodium	1351 mg

* Percent Daily Values are based on a 2,000 calorie diet.

Chicken Salad

Ingredients

- 4 C. cubed, cooked chicken meat
- 1 C. mayonnaise
- 1 tsp paprika
- 1 1/2 C. dried cranberries
- 1 C. diced celery
- 2 green onions, diced
- 1/2 C. minced green bell pepper
- 1 C. diced pecans
- 1 tsp seasoning salt
- ground black pepper to taste

Directions

- Get a bowl, combine: seasoned salt, paprika, and mayo. Get this mix smooth then add in: the nuts, celery, onion, bell peppers, and cranberries.
- Mix everything again then add the chicken and black pepper.
- Place the contents in the fridge for 65 mins then serve.
- Enjoy.

Amount per serving (12 total)

Timing Information:

Preparation	
Cooking	15 m
Total Time	15 m

Nutritional Information:

Calories	315 kcal
Fat	23.1 g
Carbohydrates	15.2g
Protein	13.9 g
Cholesterol	42 mg
Sodium	213 mg

* Percent Daily Values are based on a 2,000 calorie diet.

Corn Salad

Ingredients

Dressing:

- 1/2 cup mayonnaise
- 3 small green onions, thinly sliced
- 2 tablespoons white wine vinegar
- 2 tablespoons minced pickled jalapeno peppers
- 2 tablespoons minced fresh parsley
- 1 tablespoon light olive oil
- salt and ground black pepper to taste

Vegetables:

- 2 (11 ounce) cans shoepeg corn, rinsed and drained
- 1 cup halved grape tomatoes

Directions

- Get a bowl, combine: olive oil, mayo, parsley, green onion, jalapeno, and vinegar. Work the mix completely then combine in some pepper and salt.
- Now stir in your tomatoes and corn into the mayo mix. Place a covering of plastic on the bowl and put everything in the fridge for 4 hours.
- Enjoy.

Amount per serving 8

Timing Information:

Preparation	15 m
Total Time	4 h 15 m

Nutritional Information:

Calories	201 kcal
Fat	13.3 g
Carbohydrates	18g
Protein	2.4 g
Cholesterol	5 mg
Sodium	340 mg

* Percent Daily Values are based on a 2,000 calorie diet.

Ensalada de Papas Colombiana (10-Ingredient Potato Salad)

Ingredients

- 2 lb. red potatoes, cooked, peeled and cut into 1-inch cubes when cool
- 3 large carrots, peeled, cut into 1/2-inch pieces and steamed until crisp-tender, cooled
- 1/2 C. chopped red onion
- 1/4-1/2 C. chopped cilantro, depending on taste
- 3 large tomatoes, cut into 1-inch chunks

Salad Dressing

- 1/3 C. wine vinegar
- 1 tbsp oil
- 1 tsp seasoning salt (may add more to taste)
- 1 tsp sugar
- 1/4 tsp fresh ground black pepper

Directions

- In a large bowl, mix together the potato cubes, carrot pieces, chopped onions and cilantro.
- In a small bowl, add all the dressing ingredients and beat till well combined.
- Place the dressing over the salad with the tomato chunks and gently, stir to combine.
- Refrigerate to chill before serving.

Servings Per Recipe: 8

Timing Information:

Preparation	20 mins
Total Time	40 mins

Nutritional Information:

Calories	124.1
Fat	2.0g
Cholesterol	0.0mg
Sodium	43.1mg
Carbohydrates	24.8g
Protein	3.1g

* Percent Daily Values are based on a 2,000 calorie diet.

Tuna Salad

Ingredients

- 1 (7 oz.) can white tuna, drained and flaked
- 6 tbsps mayonnaise or salad dressing
- 1 tbsp Parmesan cheese
- 3 tbsps sweet pickle relish
- 1/8 tsp dried minced onion flakes
- 1/4 tsp curry powder
- 1 tbsp dried parsley
- 1 tsp dried dill weed
- 1 pinch garlic powder

Directions

- Get a bowl, combine: onion flakes, tuna, parmesan, and mayo.
- Stir the contents until they are smooth then add the garlic powder, curry powder, dill, and parsley.
- Stir the contents again to evenly distribute the spices.
- Enjoy over toasted buns or crackers.

Amount per serving (4 total)

Timing Information:

Preparation	
Cooking	10 m
Total Time	10 m

Nutritional Information:

Calories	228 kcal
Fat	17.3 g
Carbohydrates	5.3g
Protein	13.4 g
Cholesterol	24 mg
Sodium	255 mg

* Percent Daily Values are based on a 2,000 calorie diet.

Macaroni Salad

Ingredients

- 4 C. uncooked elbow macaroni
- 1 C. mayonnaise
- 1/4 C. distilled white vinegar
- 2/3 C. white sugar
- 2 1/2 tbsps prepared yellow mustard
- 1 1/2 tsps salt
- 1/2 tsp ground black pepper
- 1 large onion, diced
- 2 stalks celery, diced
- 1 green bell pepper, seeded and diced
- 1/4 C. grated carrot
- 2 tbsps diced pimento peppers

Directions

- Boil your macaroni in water and salt for 9 mins then remove the liquids.
- Get a bowl, combine: macaroni, onions, pimentos, celery, carrots, black pepper, mayo, salt, green peppers, vinegar, mustard, and sugar.
- Place a covering of plastic around the bowl and put everything in the fridge for 5 hrs.
- Enjoy.

Amount per serving (10 total)

Timing Information:

Preparation	20 m
Cooking	10 m
Total Time	4 h 30 m

Nutritional Information:

Calories	390 kcal
Fat	18.7 g
Carbohydrates	49.3g
Protein	6.8 g
Cholesterol	8 mg
Sodium	529 mg

* Percent Daily Values are based on a 2,000 calorie diet.

Mesa Macaroni Salad

Ingredients

- 2 C. small shell pasta
- 1 C. mayonnaise
- 2 C. chunky salsa
- 1 tbsp chopped fresh cilantro
- 6 green onions, chopped
- 1 C. cooked corn
- 1 C. sliced black olives
- 1 red pepper, chopped
- 1/2 tsp onion salt
- 1/4 tsp cayenne pepper

Directions

- In a large pan of the lightly salted boiling water, prepare the pasta according to the package's directions.
- Drain well.
- In a large bowl add the remaining ingredients and mix till well combined.
- Add the pasta and toss to coat.
- Refrigerate to chill before serving.

Servings Per Recipe: 4

Timing Information:

Preparation	10 mins
Total Time	20 mins

Nutritional Information:

Calories	534.8
Fat	24.8g
Cholesterol	15.2mg
Sodium	1501.3mg
Carbohydrates	72.7g
Protein	10.9g

* Percent Daily Values are based on a 2,000 calorie diet.

Maque Choux (Native American Style Corn Salad)

Ingredients

- 6 ears corn, husked and cleaned
- 2 tablespoons vegetable oil
- 1 large onion, thinly sliced
- 1 cup green bell pepper, chopped
- 1 large fresh tomato, chopped
- 1/4 cup milk
- salt to taste
- cayenne pepper
- 1/4 cup chopped green onions
- 8 strips crisply cooked turkey bacon, crumbled

Directions

- Remove the kernels of corn from your ears into a bowl. Slice the ears again to get the milk into the same bowl.
- Get your oil hot in a frying pan then combine in your green pepper, and onion. Stir fry the mix for 7 mins then combine in the milk, corn, and tomatoes. Stir everything then set the heat to low, and let the mix gently cook for 22 mins while stirring often. But do not let the mix get so hot that begin to boil.
- Now add some cayenne and salt then set the heat lower and place a lid on the pan. Let everything cook for 7 more minx then add the bacon and green onions.
- Enjoy.

Amount per serving 6

Timing Information:

Preparation	35 m
Cooking	30 m
Total Time	1 h 5 m

Nutritional Information:

Calories	211 kcal
Fat	11.1 g
Carbohydrates	22.8g
Protein	8.6 g
Cholesterol	14 mg
Sodium	371 mg

* Percent Daily Values are based on a 2,000 calorie diet.

Ceviche Guatemala Style

Ingredients

- 4 large tomatoes, diced
- 2 lbs medium shrimp, peeled and deveined
- 1 onion, diced
- 1 bunch cilantro, diced
- 1 jalapeno, diced
- 12 lemons, squeezed
- 8 tbsp ketchup
- 2 tsp Worcestershire sauce
- salt and pepper

Directions

- In a pan of boiling water, blanch the shrimp for about 5 minutes.
- Transfer into the bowl of ice cold water.
- Strain when cooled.
- Transfer the shrimps into the bowl.
- Add lemon juice and refrigerate to marinate for about 2 hours.
- Add salt, pepper, ketchup, Worcestershire sauce, onion, tomatoes, chilies and cilantro and refrigerate to marinate for about 2 hours.
- Serve with some nice crackers.

Amount per serving: 4

Timing Information:

Preparation	30 mins:
Total Time	24 hrs 30 mins

Nutritional Information:

Calories	238.1
Fat	2.8g
Cholesterol	286.4mg
Sodium	1648.7mg
Carbohydrates	20.0g
Protein	33.5g

* Percent Daily Values are based on a 2,000 calorie diet.

Chapter 8: Burgers and Veggie Burgers

White Steak Burgers

Ingredients

- 1 lb. fresh mushrooms, about 6 C. chopped finely
- 1 large onion, minced
- 2 slices white bread, finely diced
- 2 tbsps steak sauce
- 2 egg whites or 1 egg
- Salt
- Ground black pepper

Directions

- Place a large skillet on medium heat. Grease it with oil or cooking spray. Add the onion with mushroom and sauté them for 6 min. Add the bread dices with steak sauce. Sauté them for 1 min
- Turn off the heat. Place the mix aside to lose heat.
- Get a mixing bowl: Add the eggs and mix them well. Add the onion mix with salt and pepper. Mix them well. Shape the mix into 6 burgers.
- Place a large skillet on medium heat. Heat in it a splash of oil. Add the burgers and cook them for 8 min on each side.
- Assemble your burgers with your favorite toppings. Serve them right away.
- Enjoy.

Amount per serving: 6

Timing Information:

Preparation	20 mins
Total Time	30 mins

Nutritional Information:

Calories	54.5
Fat	0.5g
Cholesterol	0.0mg
Sodium	65.6mg
Carbohydrates	9.1g
Protein	4.4g

* Percent Daily Values are based on a 2,000 calorie diet.

Grilled Mozzarella Burger

Ingredients

- 1 tbsp balsamic vinegar
- 1 tbsp extra virgin olive oil
- Salt and pepper to taste
- 4 thick slices tomato
- 1 1/3 lbs lean ground beef
- 1 tbsp tomato paste
- 1/4 C. chopped fresh basil
- 1/4 C. grated Parmesan cheese
- 1 clove garlic, minced
- 1/4 tsp black pepper
- 4 oz. fresh mozzarella cheese, sliced
- 4 hamburger buns split

Directions

- Before you do anything preheat the grill.
- Get a small mixing bowl: Add the balsamic vinegar, oil, salt, and pepper. Whisk them well. Toss it with the tomato slices. Place them aside.
- Get a mixing bowl: Add the beef, tomato paste, basil, Parmesan cheese, garlic, and 1/4 tsp pepper. Combine them well. Shape the mix into 4 burgers.
- Grill the burgers for 6 min on each side. Place the mozzarella cheese slices on the burgers while they are hot and let them rest until the cheese melts slightly. Top them with tomato mix.
- Serve your burgers right away.
- Enjoy.

Amount per serving 4

Timing Information:

Preparation	10 m
Cooking	15 min for 6 min on
Total Time	30 m

Nutritional Information:

Calories	561 kcal
Fat	31.6 g
Carbohydrates	25.4g
Protein	40.6 g
Cholesterol	132 mg
Sodium	485 mg

* Percent Daily Values are based on a 2,000 calorie diet.

Chili Romano Burgers

Ingredients

- 1 (19 ounce) cans Romano beans, drained
- 1 egg
- 1/2 C. dry breadcrumbs
- 1/4 C. chili sauce
- 1 green onion, chopped

Directions

- Add the 3/4 of the black bean then press it with a potato masher or fork until it becomes well mashed. Add the rest of the ingredients. Mix them well. Shape the mix into 4 burger cakes.
- Place a large skillet on medium heat. Add the oil and heat it. Cook the burgers for 7 min on each side.
- Assemble your burgers with your favorite toppings. Serve them right away.
- Enjoy.

Amount per serving: 4

Timing Information:

Preparation	10 mins
Total Time	20 mins

Nutritional Information:

Calories	110.3
Fat	2.1g
Cholesterol	46.5mg
Sodium	1694.2mg
Carbohydrates	18.1g
Protein	4.9g

* Percent Daily Values are based on a 2,000 calorie diet.

GRILLED COTTAGE SANDWICH

Ingredients

- 1 C. cottage cheese (I use no or low fat)
- 1/2 tsp seasoning salt
- 1/2 tsp Worcestershire sauce
- 1 1/2 lbs ground beef

Directions

- Before you do anything preheat the grill.
- Get a mixing bowl: Add all the ingredients and mix them well. Shape the mix into 6 burgers. Grill them for 7 min one each side.
- Assemble your burgers with your favorite toppings.
- Enjoy.

Amount per serving: 6

Timing Information:

Total Time	10 mins
Cook Time	20 mins

Nutritional Information:

Calories	278.4
Fat	18.5g
Cholesterol	83.0mg
Sodium	206.8mg
Carbohydrates	1.2g
Protein	24.9g

* Percent Daily Values are based on a 2,000 calorie diet.

Braggs' Oat Burgers

Ingredients

- 1 tbsp extra virgin olive oil
- 1/2 C. onion, finely chopped
- 1/4 C. grated carrot
- 1/4 C. celery, finely chopped
- 1/4 C. grated zucchini or 1/4 C. summer squash
- 1 C. cooked brown rice
- 1 1/2 C. quick oats
- 1/2 tsp garlic powder
- 1/2 tsp cumin powder
- 1/8 tsp cayenne powder
- 1 tbsp nutritional yeast flakes
- 1 (12 1/3 ounce) packages firm tofu or 1 (12 1/3 ounce) packages extra firm tofu
- 1 tsp all-purpose vegetable
- 1/2 C. water
- 2 tbsps Braggs liquid aminos or 2 tbsps soy sauce
- Breadcrumbs, for coating the patties

Directions

- Before you do anything preheat the oven on 375 F. Place a large skillet on medium heat. Heat the olive oil in it. Add the onion, carrot, celery and zucchini then cook them for 5 min. Turn off the heat.
- Stir in the rice, oats and seasonings. Combine them well. Stir in the tofu and press it with a fork until it becomes finely mashed.
- Get a mixing bowl: Add the water with aminos. Mix them well. Add the tofu mix and combine them well. Shape the mix into 8 burger cakes. Coat them with the bread crumbs.
- Place the burgers on a lined up baking sheet. Cook them in the oven for 16 min. Flip them and grease them with a cooking spray. Cook them for 22 min. Let them rest for 6 min.
- Assemble your burgers with your favorite toppings. Serve them right away. Enjoy.

Amount per serving: 8

Timing Information:

Preparation	20 mins
Total Time	1 hr.

Nutritional Information:

Calories	143.3
Fat	4.8g
Cholesterol	0.0mg
Sodium	13.0mg
Carbohydrates	18.9g
Protein	7.4g

* Percent Daily Values are based on a 2,000 calorie diet.

Dreamy Cheesy Burger

Ingredients

- 2 lbs ground beef
- 1 (1 oz.) package spring vegetable soup mix, like Knorr
- 1/2 C. minced red onion
- 1 1/4 C. shredded four cheese blends
- 6 hamburger buns split
- Shredded lettuce
- Sliced tomatoes
- Pimento stuffed olive

Directions

- Before you do anything preheat the grill.
- Get a mixing bowl: Add the beef, soup mix, red onion and 1/2 C. cheese. Mix them well. Shape the mix into 6 burgers.
- Grill the patties for 8 min on each side. Place 2 tbsps of cheese on top of each burger then cook them for 2 min until the cheese melts.
- Assemble your burgers with lettuce and tomato slices. Serve them right away.
- Enjoy.

Amount per serving: 6

Timing Information:

Total Time	15 mins
Cook Time	30 mins

Nutritional Information:

Calories	466.0
Fat	24.7g
Cholesterol	102.9mg
Sodium	623.8mg
Carbohydrates	25.4g
Protein	32.8g

* Percent Daily Values are based on a 2,000 calorie diet.

Peanut Butter Burgers

Ingredients

- 1 C. textured vegetable protein
- 1/4 C. quick-cooking rolled oats
- 1/2 tsp dried oregano
- 1/2 tsp dried basil, flakes
- 1/2 tsp dried parsley flakes
- 1/2 tsp onion, granules
- 1/2 tsp garlic granules
- 1/4 tsp mustard powder
- 3/4 C. water (almost-boiling)
- 2 tbsps organic ketchup
- 2 tbsps soy sauce (or tamari or Bragg's)
- 1 tbsp creamy peanut butter (can also use tahini or any other nut or seed butter)
- 1/4 C. whole wheat pastry flour
- 1 tbsp nutritional yeast

Directions

- Get a mixing bowl: Add the water with oregano, basil, parsley flakes, onion, garlic granules, and mustard powder, oats and TVP chunks. Combine them well.
- Stir in the ketchup and soy sauce. Mix them well. Fold in the nut butter with whole-wheat pastry flour and nutritional yeast. Combine them well. Shape the mix into 4 burger cakes.
- Place a large skillet on medium heat. Heat in it a splash of oil. Add the burgers and cook them for 7 min on each side.
- Assemble your burgers with your favorite toppings. Serve them right away.
- Enjoy.

Amount per serving: 4

Timing Information:

Preparation	10 mins
Total Time	25 mins

Nutritional Information:

Calories	93.4
Fat	2.8g
Cholesterol	0.0mg
Sodium	608.6mg
Carbohydrates	13.7g
Protein	5.1g

* Percent Daily Values are based on a 2,000 calorie diet.

Barbecue Oat Burgers

Ingredients

- 3 onions, chopped
- 2 tbsps minced fresh garlic
- 1/2 tsp cayenne pepper (or to taste)
- 1 tsp dried basil
- 1 tsp dried oregano
- 3 -5 tbsps olive oil
- 1 1/2 lbs ground turkey (use white and dark)
- 1/4 C. favorite barbecue sauce
- 3 tbsps quick-cooking oats
- 1/2 C. grated cheddar cheese or 1/2 C. mozzarella cheese, packed
- 1/3 C. grated parmesan cheese
- 3 tbsps milk (or use half and half cream)
- 2 tsps seasoning salt
- 1 tsp black pepper (add in more if desired)
- 1/3 C. dried breadcrumbs (you will most likely need more)

Directions

- Place a large skillet on medium heat. Heat the oil in it. Add the onions with cayenne, oregano and basil. Cook them for 6 min. add the garlic and cook them for 1 min.
- Place the mix in a mixing bowl and place it aside to lose heat. Add the turkey, BBQ sauce, oats, shredded cheese, Parmesan cheese, milk, seasoning salt, pepper. Mix them well.
- Stir in 1/3 C. dried bread crumbs and mix them again. Add some milk if the mix is too dry. Shape the mix into 9 burgers. And wrap them in a piece of foil. Refrigerate them for 8 h.
- Before you do anything preheat the grill.
- Grill the burgers for 7 min on each side. Assemble with your favorite toppings. Serve your burgers right away. Enjoy.

Amount per serving: 10

Timing Information:

Total Time	24 hrs.
Cook Time	24 hrs 12 mins

Nutritional Information:

Calories	219.7
Fat	13.1g
Cholesterol	63.3mg
Sodium	231.1mg
Carbohydrates	9.0g
Protein	16.0g

* Percent Daily Values are based on a 2,000 calorie diet.

Hot Chili Braggs Burgers

Ingredients

- 1/4 C. onion, grated
- 1/4 C. bell pepper, grated
- 1 1/2 C. cooked lentils
- 1/2 C. flax seed, ground
- 1/2 C. almonds
- 2 tbsps shredded carrots
- 2 tbsps shredded celery
- 1 fresh jalapenos
- 2 garlic cloves, crushed
- 2 tbsps fresh parsley, chopped
- 1 tsp olive oil
- 1 tsp Braggs liquid aminos
- 1 tbsp tomato paste
- 1 tsp dried oregano
- 1 tsp dried basil
- 1/2 tsp chili powder
- 1/2 tsp curry powder
- 1/2 tsp fresh ground black pepper
- 1/4 tsp ground red pepper

Directions

- Before you do anything preheat the oven on 350 F.
- Press the bell pepper and onion in a fine masher. Press them to remove the water coming out from them.
- Get a mixing bowl: Add the 3/4 of the lentils then press it with a potato masher or fork until it becomes well mashed.
- Add the onion and pepper mix with the rest of the ingredients. Mix them well. Place the mix aside for 1 h with the lid on. Shape the mix into 6 patties.
- Place the patties on a lined up baking sheet. Cook them in the oven for 8 min on each side.
- Assemble your burgers with your favorite toppings. Serve them right away. Enjoy.

Amount per serving: 6

Timing Information:

Preparation	15 mins
Total Time	40 mins

Nutritional Information:

Calories	219.3
Fat	12.9g
Cholesterol	0.0mg
Sodium	74.4mg
Carbohydrates	19.1g
Protein	9.9g

* Percent Daily Values are based on a 2,000 calorie diet.

Yoshida Burgers

Ingredients

- 1 lb ground beef
- 1/2 C. Yoshida gourmet sauce
- 1/4 tsp salt
- 1/4 tsp fresh ground black pepper
- 4 oz. blue cheese
- 4 hamburger buns

Directions

- Before you do anything preheat the grill.
- Get a mixing bowl: Combine the beef with gourmet sauce, salt, and pepper well. Shape the mix into 8 thin burgers. Place the oz. of blue cheese on 4 patties.
- Cover them with the other 4 patties and pinch the edges to seal the edges. Cook them on the grill for 8 min on each side.
- Assemble your burgers with your favorite toppings. Serve your burgers right away.
- Enjoy.

Amount per serving: 4

Timing Information:

Total Time	15 mins
Cook Time	25 mins

Nutritional Information:

Calories	464.1
Fat	27.0g
Cholesterol	98.3mg
Sodium	821.7mg
Carbohydrates	22.0g
Protein	31.2g

* Percent Daily Values are based on a 2,000 calorie diet.

Latin Salsa Burgers

Ingredients

- 1 (15 ounce) cans black beans, rinsed & drained
- 1 C. rice, cooked
- 1/4 C. onion, finely chopped
- 2 tbsps salsa
- 1 egg, beaten

Directions

- Get a mixing bowl: Add the black bean then press it with a potato masher or fork until it becomes well mashed. Add the rest of the ingredients. Mix them well. Shape the mix into 4 burger cakes.
- Place a skillet on medium heat. Add the oil and heat. Add the burger cakes and cook them for 6 min on each side.
- Assemble your burgers with your favorite toppings. Serve them right away.
- Enjoy.

Amount per serving: 4

Timing Information:

Preparation	10 mins
Total Time	20 mins

Nutritional Information:

Calories	303.8
Fat	1.9g
Cholesterol	52.8mg
Sodium	1118.0mg
Carbohydrates	59.0g
Protein	111.9g

* Percent Daily Values are based on a 2,000 calorie diet.

Worcestershire Pastrami Burger

Ingredients

- 1 3/4 lbs ground chuck
- 1 egg (optional)
- 2 tsps Worcestershire sauce
- 4 hamburger buns
- 4 slices pastrami
- 4 slices mozzarella cheese
- 1/2 tsp salt
- 1/4 tsp pepper
- Mustard (optional)
- Ketchup (optional)
- Mayonnaise (optional)
- 4 lettuce leaves
- 4 tomatoes, slices
- 4 onions, slices
- 4 pickles, slices

Directions

- Before you do anything preheat the grill. Toast the burger buns and place them aside.
- Get a mixing bowl: Add the chuck with egg, Worcestershire sauce, salt, and pepper. Combine them well. Shape the mix into 4 burgers.
- Grill the burgers for 7 min on each side. Lay the pastrami on the burgers buns then top it with burgers, cheese and veggies slices. Serve your burgers right away.
- Enjoy.

Amount per serving: 4

Timing Information:

Total Time	10 mins
Cook Time	25 mins

Nutritional Information:

Calories	843.6
Fat	46.8g
Cholesterol	208.0mg
Sodium	2033.1mg
Carbohydrates	40.2g
Protein	63.4g

* Percent Daily Values are based on a 2,000 calorie diet.

Quaker Corn Burgers

Ingredients

- 1 C. cooked pureed white beans, including some liquid or 1 C. beans, of your choice
- 1 C. cooked brown rice
- 1/2 C. uncooked Quaker multigrain cereal (or oats)
- 1 C. cornbread stuffing mix
- 1 tbsp parsley
- 1/2 C. chopped onion
- 1 tbsp soy sauce

Directions

- Get a mixing bowl: Add the all the ingredients. Mix them well. Shape the mix into 2 burger cakes.
- Place a skillet on medium heat. Add the oil and heat. Add the burger cakes and cook them for 5 min on each side.
- Assemble your burgers with your favorite toppings. Serve them right away.
- Enjoy.

Amount per serving: 1

Timing Information:

Preparation	15 mins
Total Time	27 mins

Nutritional Information:

Calories	112.2
Fat	0.5g
Cholesterol	0.0mg
Sodium	205.1mg
Carbohydrates	22.0g
Protein	5.2g

* Percent Daily Values are based on a 2,000 calorie diet.

Classical London Sirloin Burger

Ingredients

- 1 lb ground beef
- 1/4 C. Lea & Perrins Worcestershire Sauce
- 1/2 C. sharp aged cheddar cheese, shredded
- 1/4 C. chopped slightly crisp cooked bacon

Directions

- Before you do anything preheat the grill.
- Get a mixing bowl: Add the all the ingredients. Mix them well. Shape the mix into 3 4 burgers.
- Grill them for 6 to 8 min on each side. Serve your burgers with your favorite toppings.
- Enjoy.

Amount per serving: 4

Timing Information:

Total Time	10 mins
Cook Time	22 mins

Nutritional Information:

Calories	341.8
Fat	23.8g
Cholesterol	97.5mg
Sodium	449.3mg
Carbohydrates	3.6g
Protein	26.5g

* Percent Daily Values are based on a 2,000 calorie diet.

Appendix I: Spice Mixes

Mango & Raisin Chutney

Ingredients

- 1 kg very firm mango
- 2 C. sugar
- 625 ml vinegar
- 1 (5 cm) pieces ginger, peeled
- 4 cloves garlic, peeled
- 2 -4 tsps chili powder
- 4 tsps mustard seeds
- 8 tsps salt
- 1 C. raisins or 1 C. sultana

Directions

- Peel the mango and then remove the pit and chop it.
- In a pan, add sugar and vinegar, leaving about 20ml and simmer, stirring occasionally for about 10 minutes.
- Meanwhile in a food processor, add remaining vinegar, garlic and ginger and pulse till a paste forms.
- Transfer the paste into a pan and simmer, stirring continuously for about 10 minutes.
- Stir in the mango and remaining ingredients and simmer, stirring occasionally for about 25 minutes or till desired thickness of chutney. Transfer the chutney into hot sterilized jars and seal tightly and keep aside to cool.
- This chutney can be stored in dark place for about 1 year but remember to refrigerate after opening.

Amount per serving: 1

Timing Information:

Preparation	20 mins
Total Time	1 hr 5 mins

Nutritional Information:

Calories	627.2
Fat	2.1g
Cholesterol	0.0mg
Sodium	3748.7mg
Carbohydrates	153.4g
Protein	4.2g

* Percent Daily Values are based on a 2,000 calorie diet.

Cajun Spice Mix

This Cajun style seasoning can be used for meats but one of its best uses is for potatoes which you should bake in the oven.

Ingredients

- 2 tsps salt
- 2 tsps garlic powder
- 2 1/2 tsps paprika
- 1 tsp ground black pepper
- 1 tsp onion powder
- 1 tsp cayenne pepper
- 1 1/4 tsps dried oregano
- 1 1/4 tsps dried thyme
- 1/2 tsp red pepper flakes (optional)

Directions

- Get a bowl, evenly mix or sift: red pepper flakes, salt, thyme, garlic powder, oregano, paprika, cayenne, onion powder, and black pepper.
- Get a good container that is airtight and store your mix.

Timing Information:

Preparation	Cooking	Total Time
5 m		5 m

Nutritional Information:

Calories	6 kcal
Fat	0.1 g
Carbohydrates	1.2g
Protein	0.2 g
Cholesterol	0 mg
Sodium	388 mg

* Percent Daily Values are based on a 2,000 calorie diet.

THANKS FOR READING! JOIN THE CLUB AND KEEP ON COOKING WITH 6 MORE COOKBOOKS....

http://bit.ly/1TdrStv

 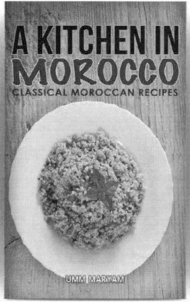 

To grab the box sets simply follow the link mentioned above, or tap one of book covers.

This will take you to a page where you can simply enter your email address and a PDF version of the box sets will be emailed to you.

Hope you are ready for some serious cooking!

http://bit.ly/1TdrStv

Come On...
Let's Be Friends :)

We adore our readers and love connecting with them socially.

Like BookSumo on Facebook and let's get social!

Facebook

And also check out the BookSumo Cooking Blog.

Food Lover Blog

Made in the USA
San Bernardino, CA
04 December 2019